# STARTistics

A statistical sleuth reveals the inside secrets on
managing startup

SUBHASH KUMAR

ISBN 978-93-5667-275-8
© SUBHASH KUMAR 2023
Published in India 2023 by Pencil

*A brand of*
One Point Six Technologies Pvt. Ltd.
123, Building J2, Shram Seva Premises,
Wadala Truck Terminal, Wadala (E)
Mumbai 400037, Maharashtra, INDIA
**E** connect@thepencilapp.com
**W** www.thepencilapp.com

# Author biography

Subhash is an alumnus of XLRI Jamshedpur. He belongs to Bokaro Steel City in Jharkhand. He has been an entrepreneur for several things and the art of creation fascinates him.

# CONTENTS

# Preface

Let me put a disclaimer right at the beginning… you don't need to be a statistician to read the book. I have tried to come up with a view which seems to be the Minimum Variance Unbiased Estimator (MVUE) on launching Startup. MVUE simply means to choose an unbiased estimator with minimum variance. In layman's terms, it means, to choose something with less volatility or variability, or choose with consensus. The points discussed are the bare minimum to enter the Startup world. Startups are hard to succeed. Around 90% of the entrepreneurs' businesses don't see the light of the day. While more than a thousand don't survive even six months when launched.

Startups that succeed add a net worth of a few trillion, that is, the GDP of a few smaller countries. Google-parent Alphabet soared to a $1 trillion valuation, pushing the total value of the five biggest tech companies to a record $5 trillion. For some, my views on Startups may be completely biased and subjective, but it provides logical insight for budding entrepreneurs. You are free to accept or reject the hypothesis based on your understanding, but the book in the form of a hypothesis is worth your consideration. For some of you, these statistical terms scare you, don't worry we will cover them in detail from the entrepreneurial lens.

This book will help you to take manageable steps and make an informed choice. It's a roadmap that also tells you, why the art of perfection sometimes kills. There is more psychological barrier to becoming successful as an entrepreneur. Getting the fundamentals right at the beginning of a Startup will save tonnes of cash and equity!

Developing an entrepreneurial mindset and having a toolkit to overcome challenges are crucial, the book has it all. Above all the major forces for creating a successful Startup are the courage, insight, knowledge, perseverance and intensity to follow dreams. This book covers topics like, how to launch a Kickstarter campaign; How to divide the equity; What is the behavioural barrier of an entrepreneur; Why the product fails and why customers ignore the products.

**November 2022**

**Subhash            Kumar**

# 0. The Skewed Fundamentals on Startup

## *0.1 The common misconception of who an entrepreneur is?*

I am a critique of the conventional thinking on the definition of entrepreneurship. 'Entrepreneurs are innovative, intrepid and risk-takers; it's awesome.' No, it's not!! This is what most people feed their minds with while the truth differs. Media portray entrepreneurs as charismatic leaders, game changers and innovators. Joseph Schumpeter (1965) defined entrepreneurs as 'individuals who exploit market opportunity through technical and organizational innovation'. While the definition is not wrong, it does not portray an accurate picture of what entrepreneurship is.

The inside secret is, that it is hard. Entrepreneurship can be desirous, unglamorous, discouraging, hopeless and embarrassing. These traits are key to a successful entrepreneur. Entrepreneurship is not about rewards or equity but the fight for self-confidence, perseverance, non-negotiable commitment, passion, work ethics, charisma, vision, persuasion, leadership and effective personal attributes that are difficult to teach.

What media offers is a seductive and romantic view. It's certainly not the only description of an entrepreneur. An entrepreneur is someone who is in pursuit of opportunities beyond the resources that she currently controls. It is about someone who doesn't know how to do things but will look for ways to do things with constraints. It is more about strategy and execution. I think it's time to move on from the generalist notion, that an entrepreneur is 'someone who develops new products, finds markets, and innovates products'.

### 0.2 Why become an entrepreneur?
*Entrepreneurs are happy people!*

One of the reasons entrepreneurs follow their passion and start a business is because it will make them happy, and may not be wealthier. The satisfaction at the end of the day is long-lasting. When following the path of entrepreneurship people earn (as much as 30%) less in their lifetime than they would have if they had been in jobs. What motivates people to start a business is not money. A lot of studies show that entrepreneurship is an opportunity to learn, create one's own responsibility and be recognised for achievements. So, money is not a powerful motivator and after some time money, status and compensation are the by-products of being happy. The second reason to pursue entrepreneurship is to control the ability to determine, what to do when to do it, and whom to do it with… And ultimately choose what you do with your life? The control gives deep inner satisfaction at the end of the day.

Entrepreneurship gives a sense of entitlement. Entrepreneurship is figuring out the source of getting funds, getting the first employee, selling products, and developing a new product that the world aspires for. An MBA degree does not teach enough and there is a lot to learn from fellow entrepreneurs and high school dropouts who have successful startups. There is an opportunity to learn even from an onion seller in Nasik, Maharashtra, who has no degree but he knows how the supply chain works and makes millions in a single day's transaction.

As an MBA you can get into Goldman Sachs, but if you want to be the Goldman, it's more than an impediment. MBA degrees are famous and are a cash cow for institutes and there is too much hype around it, but to be honest, most of the premier institutes just act as placement cells. The moment the placement facility ends, the reality will pop up about how many exactly there are takers for these pieces of degree paper. Of course, there is a curriculum for entrepreneurship, but choose to learn by doing, rather than getting into classroom lectures. India is too theoretically inclined and most of the fundamentals taught have become obsolete and are of no use when entering the journey! Now, if you are already pursuing an MBA, you can add synergy to the concepts taught by just starting with an idea and incorporating a new venture.

The career satisfaction among the founders is the highest among all careers including finance, consulting, consumer, non-profit, health, manufacturing, etc. Many want to start a new business but, a corporate job and a monthly salary are addictive. However, in a corporate job, you live at the mercy of bosses for a single day's leave, work to do and even people with whom you interact! Those who have the bug to start, do it sooner or later. The backbiting culture, mistrust, repetitive copy and paste job and office politics are just some of the common things that push many towards entrepreneurs. The truth of corporate culture impostures the perks, but nobody talks about the hard truth.

## *0.3 Job Vs Entrepreneurship*

Entrepreneurship versus a job is comparable to a pity boat versus a battleship. When someone who is working for someone else is in the battleship, as opposed to when you are an entrepreneur, you are sitting in a pity boat. But, in a battleship, you have no idea where your ship is going; you have no idea what decisions will be made on the bridge. It can be hit by a torpedo at any time and you are dead! But when you are in a pity boat you can look around and see from where the storm is coming and take decisions about which way to go; you are somewhat in control.

The one rule for business is to never have one employee, one vendor, or one customer. But when you work for somebody else you violate that rule. If you have one customer, and when that one customer decides that he does not need you anymore, you are totally out of business; you have to go find another business… this is true in the case of most jobs.

## 0.4 A startup is a game that founders play

*It's a game of founders, don't get tricked by the money, IPO and the product. It's a story of your life.*

**This game of Maze is amazing, but it never ends!**

A startup is a careful alignment of several moving parts. The knowledge of these moving parts is a must-have to succeed. For example, a surgeon cannot operate without understating patient diagnostics; similarly, startups cannot deliver without understanding the moving parts, i.e., people, markets, and business model. Building startups is a messy process which tests the spirit of entrepreneurs. Startups are unstructured, unorganized, deeply involved and unplanned which totally differentiates them from large established firms. The learning through the actual decision-making and trade-off between the choices, ultimately drive the startups.

A startup is a game that starts with courage, and an idea. As we have existence, we grow, breathe, eat and sleep, and so do the companies. Like all living things, companies need to be nurtured, developed and shaped. Companies also compete, evolve, mature, and die like the life cycle of a human being. The four stages of the Product Life Cycle (PLC) start from the introduction and move on to growth, maturity and decline. For example, look at the Bajaj scooter or Onida television sets that we had in the '90s. They don't exist now. These products have completed their life cycle. The creator of a company has the ultimate responsibility to lead. Like every person, a company has a name, a registered address, domicile and occupation. The name of a company is clear by itself; the company domicile is the state it belongs to, in the form of a registered office. The two most important documents of the company are the Memorandum of Association and the Article of Associations that decide the nature and extent of the business venture.

The legal status decides which rule or law you have to abide by. You can form a sole proprietorship, partnership, private limited company, limited liability partnership or a public limited company. Each legal form has different obligations and complexity to be enforced. For example, both a private limited company and a public limited company have mandatory auditing every year; they conduct Annual General Meetings (AGM) and file their taxes. While the sole proprietor and partnership firms have to file their taxes every year, the sole proprietor and partnership firms are not considered separate from the owner. This means, that if the founder dies so does the entity.

Public and private companies on the other hand are separate legal entities, and someone can take over and run them even after the demise of the founder. If humans die, they stop the work, but the companies can keep going even if the promoter dies. This basically means that the companies are separate from the promoter and someone else can take the lead role after the death of the founder member. Companies die only with the windup of the company through the resolution by the board. You need two things to start a business; a CA and a lawyer, with some money physically on the paper.

**They are exactly the same, I don't think a coin toss can fix that!**

The entrepreneur starts the inception of the company with the registration certificate given by the Registrar of Companies. He infuses capital, and human resources and gives the initial shape to the company. In return, he gets a chunk of shares which, to be honest, is worth nothing and is just a piece of paper when started. The entrepreneur buys shares of his own company with a face value which could be around five, ten, or twenty rupees or what the compliance offer is considered fit compared to the actual value of the company. The Founder/s form an entity put in the money and buy all (100%) of its stakes. If there are more people in incepting the company like co-founders, then the stake is divided as agreed between them.

The Founders are on a quest to find a unique solution or invent a better way of doing business through making a better product or innovating technology. The founder infuses capital into the company with the expectation that when things move, he will get a better value price for his shares. There is a trade-off of time, risk, capital and commitment with the future benefits. The entrepreneur often swaps shares with employees, VCs and co-founders and increases the team which works towards a shared vision. The newly born organization need funds, organizational structure, and a unique product. The rule of the game is developed by the founders. All the internal constituents and processes are developed by the director or CEO who initially is the founder or they can also bring a professional CEO. The nature of business is not under the control of the director. The director has limited powers and cannot supersede the control of the chairperson of the board.

The venture capitalist plays a major role by providing blood to the business and putting skin in the game. He also has the power to alter the business as desired, depending on the shares and board members. Any external money in the business also comes with losing control but it is better to be in the game by giving the much-needed cash than losing it. Venture Capitalists (VC) take a stake of 25 to 40% in the company. VCs are professionals; they invest to earn from the exit in a time horizon, usually, a span of five to ten years by selling the shares at a higher price than they purchased. Initial Public Offering (IPO) is the ultimate destination of a Startup. Only when a company has a certain standing in the market, can it issue an IPO. The public can buy and sell the shares of the company and the risk and reward are not just limited to a handful of people but are distributed among the masses. After that, the IPO entrepreneur can sell the stocks at the market rate, which is usually higher than what he had initially invested per share. They don't have to worry much about success or failure at this point in time.

## 0.5 Linear Output

**After 35 years of career, finally I discovered the secret image that enlightens mind. These two outliers are just extraordinary.**

We like to look at our world as linear, in two dimensions. For example, working for eight hours a day. However, just hard work is not a substitute for building a three-dimensional system to achieve your goal. A guy working in the grocery store is just running as hard as if not harder than you and me. What is the output is he getting? What you work on and who you work with will give an added dimension to what you are passionate about. It is very important to choose the 'what' and 'whom' well in order to get greater output.

We get linear output by working the same amount of time i.e., eight hours daily. Most entrepreneurs think that productivity is linear while, in reality, it is three-dimensional. The way to increase the output is to choose what you do, who you do it with and how you do it. Who you do it with, is way more important than how hard you work! The right way to get the best output is to work like a lion while some people graze all day. We should work like an athlete… We should train hard, sprint and then take rest. We should reassess and create a feedback loop to strengthen the system.

## 0.6 Why a business fails

*The stat is simple, just don't clash with your co-founder. It's like a live-in relationship. You feel like you should get 'divorced' daily! But, while some things settle in bed at night some will wait for the morning.*

Most businesses fail, the reason being that the co-founder's relationship issues are not handled maturely. In a research article "What do venture capitalists do?" Michael Gorman and William A. Sahlman, say approximately 65% of businesses fail due to conflict between senior management teams. This is a huge cost and burden on the entrepreneurs. Only 35% of businesses fail due to product, finance or marketing problems. Startups should handle relationships meticulously. Finding out early how to drive the key decision and have a succinct way to manage conflict can save a lot of time, resources and effort. Often things go bad, there is a need to develop a mechanism through which they can be resolved. In most cases, relationships are one of the prime factors that sabotage everything, and people end up blaming each other. Whether it is the relationships between co-founders or internal management or investors. The key to a successful company is to manage conflicts and have fun. Starting up is hard in itself don't make it harder.

It looks terrible when people confront each other. Co-founders decide to come on the same platform for the same goal, but instead of complementing each other, the individual goals supersede the common vision. Every person has a different motive and values. People bring different personalities to the table and that's what strengthens the company. When people confront each other, the strength becomes a weakness and ends with benefitting nobody, neither the individual nor the company. The importance of a co-founder cannot be overemphasized. Two people can create a miracle and achieve the unexpected. The company is important otherwise co-founders will be exhausted alone.

In this research article, I have discussed a sure success formula that will make a company bankrupt, which is just to let the co-founder fight with each other.

*How are the decisions to be made?*
The obvious thing to consider before getting into a Startup is, how decisions are to be made. Who gets what percentage of equity may be a deciding factor of who will decide what. Getting the decisions early about the equity distribution is good. The other option to make decisions is through setting up a board of advisors. The complex and important matters could be left to the board to fix, while the day-to-day things could be managed by the founders.

The founding team should also look for, what task each co-founder will handle. What will happen if any co-founder leaves the company? Will it be appropriate to leave with all the shares, leaving the partners in a deadlock? I guess nobody wants that, at least before starting the company your intentions should not be so! A startup is a rollercoaster ride with excitement, sometimes one person enjoys the ride but another may not. The commitment and motivation can vary, depending upon the complexity of the relationship. For a startup, it is very difficult to manage a free rider who is not fully committed to a shared vision.

Can any one of the co-founders be fired? Who will fire him or her? What could be the reasons? How much should be the remuneration drawn and how to manage conflict, are a few other things to think about carefully. The company should have a mechanism to check what's good for the business. The core values like culture are of prime importance. Culture is not something that can be changed in a few days. Checking the personal goals is important as one founder may try to run the company just for profit while another may want a social mission for the greater good. Deciding on the values and motivations early helps.

## 0.7 Founders Choices

*It's Alice in wonderland. You've got to do it because inaction is better than no action.*

### Diversity in Startups

There is a tradeoff between the less diverse and diverse employees in companies. Companies that have similar employee backgrounds act quicker and are more likely to stay together and move faster. The less diverse teams are better in communication and understanding and the teams can be built upon if you have an exploitative nature of the company. A company that is diverse increases valuation by a few percentages for each diverse person. There is a strong trade-off between diversity and valuation. Research also shows that more diversified higher management teams are valued at higher, i.e., around 7 to 12% more. However, diverse teams are also likely to fall apart quickly. The companies can either be exploratory or exploitative in nature. More diversity is better for exploratory companies, that is, the companies that look to develop new products and design innovative solutions and technologies.

*Rich versus king tradeoff*

People start businesses to gain freedom and to make money. Many want to become rich quickly, but others prefer to be their own boss. It's very difficult for the founder to have both and there is often a tradeoff. Rich versus king is another aspect that is reflected by Noam Wasserman in his article "Rich versus King: The Entrepreneur's Dilemma". Here rich are interpreted as the founder who prefers cash by giving the equity; while the king is more about the control of the company and leaving the cash aside giving no equity. Does the founder have to make a decision about how much control you want over the company? King founders may fall short of cash where the organization is difficult to run. If founders want to maintain control, it is very difficult for a startup to raise funds, get employees and grow quickly. If companies have to maintain growth, then they have to give control, as investors also come with better skills, advice and managerial decisions.

For some companies, maintaining control has been an important task because they started the company with a vision for the same purpose. Neil Blumenthal is a co-founder of Warby Parker, a transformative lifestyle brand, a socially conscious business that offers designer eyewear. He had two reasons to start, one was to radically transform the eyewear and the second was to build a company that is scalable, and profitable without charging a premium. One of the fears they had was that, if the investor takes control, they might deprioritize the social mission. The way to maintain control is by having a different voting structure. They also chose the investor whom they thought would feel excited and at the same time also preserve the social mission.

Those companies who gave up control in lieu of cash are more successful, they end up having a smaller pie in a highly valued company. Founders who choose control and don't prefer to dilute the company and take external money, end up being king and their company is half as valuable as the rich founders. The figure given below shows the tradeoff between rich vs king tradeoff. The most valued companies are those that choose to give up both the position of the CEO and board control. Next are those founders who only maintained the CEO position and thereafter we have those who retained the control of the board; lastly, we have those who have retained both the position of the CEO and board control. The share of evaluation drops by 50% for companies that choose to have tight control on the board and CEO's position. Also, king founders are under-resourced and attract less skilled employees, if not willing to give up their control.

*The Founder's Dilemmas by Noam Wasserman*

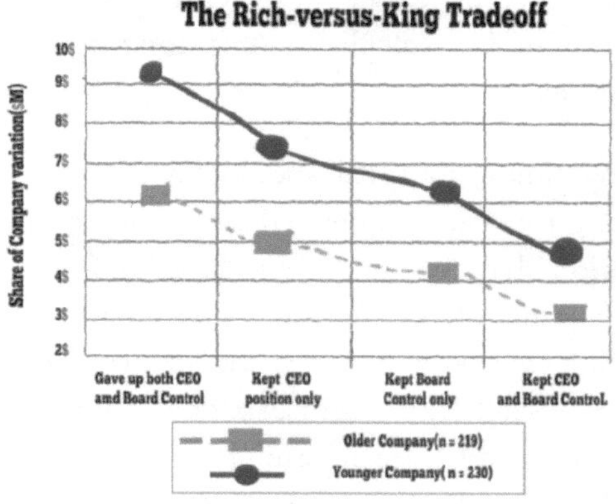



There is a handful of companies that have king founders, and it is very hard to know how the king founders perform. They are exceptional people who can really grow a company from nothing to something huge, Nitin Kamath of Zerodha is one example. All super kings and founders fail and a small percentage of them succeed like Steve Jobs or Mark Zuckerberg.

*Funding*

*Joshua Kopelman*is known as a founder of First Round Capital (a pioneering seed-stage venture fund that led the seed round in Uber). When they started raising money in round B, they had multiple term sheets and he ended up choosing the one which valued his company 20% less than the highest in the term sheet. The reason is the belief that a set of experiences and connections could add value and increase the likelihood of a good outcome far more than the highest price investor. It turns out *Kopelman*was right when they sold the company to *eBay*. The investor played a key role and the 20% delusion was a good trade. So, founders can become either short-term greedy or long-term greedy, there is a calculus to this, long-term greed is the rich approach.

When raising funds, the goal should be to get investors without giving too much equity. Also, funding comes with the expectation that the investor is looking for a return. This is what is usually not found mentioned in the term sheet. In other words, how big is the size of the exit for the investor? Usually, investors expect five times or ten times the amount they are investing in. To some degree when founders sign the term sheet, they should figure out what the return expectations are. In some cases, taking a lot of money at a high price might reduce the odds of success. Think of it as an *express train versus a local one*! When an investor is investing a lot of cash, they are buying a ticket to the express train. There is another timesheet that takes less money, which will still reach the same destination, but the door will open on both sides, multiple times along the way, both ways. So sometimes taking less money may increase the odds, because it gives an entrepreneur and investor more options to get out of the train.

The funding becomes crucial also, what investors bring to the table apart from the funds i.e., expertise and mentorship are as much needed. The investors in return for funding, take a big chunk of equity which could be the deciding factor when it comes to controlling the company in future. Giving too much equity can harm the company, as the founder will lose complete control over the company and cannot move the company in the desired direction when needed. Also, less equity is left for employees, future investors and founders themselves.

On the other hand, giving very less equity means that the fund raised are not enough to sustain the company. Outside investors can also bring the network whether it is partners, funders or employees. Raising the valuation after each round could be beneficial to the founders as they can show the strength of the company with growth and stability. However, a down round where the value of the company drops between the rounds can be a major concern for the funder and investors, as early-stage investors might think of overpaying the funds at limited equity.

*Hiring*

Not all employees are created equal, employees who can cope with the challenges and rise are useful. Initial hiring in a company has long-term consequences, often in the early phase, the startup founders lack the basic HR skills and are disorganized. Startups face challenges in finding good people to work with. The diversity of the social network and multiple connections make the entrepreneurs better positioned in every stage including employees. Studies have found that the differences between the individual in the middle manager role to the company performance are as high as 22%. Also, the difference between the best and worst employees in programming is more than twenty times.

*Individual Vs Group*

Founders take many decisions during the startup phase. One of them is to know who does better, individual vs group. As expected, groups do better! When starting a company in a group, three people starting up a company are better off than two people as co-founders or one person as a founder. The company valuation is also highest for those startups that have three founders, beyond three it's very difficult to manage the day-to-day operations and conflict will increase the odds. The other factor to consider is the experienced team performance versus the novice teams. The experienced team is better, as predictable. Also, novice teams do worse, if they don't raise VC funds.

## 0.8 How to divide equity?

*Don't draw for more stake, no matter how much stake you have in the company, it's just a worthless piece of paper now, nobody knows the future.*

**How much milk will you give after the lactation period?**

When choosing a co-founder, you should choose someone with whom you have good chemistry. The domain expertise that the co-founders have, can bring strength to the company. For example, one with technical knowledge with B. Tech and the other with management skills and MBA. Generally, equity splits are an awkward conversation because of a zero-sum game but it works as a lubricant in an engine.

### Startup and uncertainty

When making decisions on equity, uncertainty plays a big role. Uncertainty in terms of product development, fundraising, and co-founder conflicts are common in startups. I think the challenge is not knowing what has happened until now, but being prepared for future uncertainty. There is a famous quote by *Donald Rumsfeld. 'There are known known, there are known unknown, and there are unknown, unknown in any industry.'* 'Known known' refers to things that we are aware that we know. 'Known unknown' refers to things that we are aware of, we do not know. 'Unknown unknown' refers to things we are not aware of that we don't know. If one looks throughout history, it is the latter category that tends to be the difficult ones.

The 'known known' in a business are the facts, for example, the initial investment. The known unknown are the assumptions we make in business decisions for example future work, whose job is more important, we have to raise funding and we don't know whether we will be successful in raising funds or not. These are known unknown and the person who figures it out may get half the percentage of equity. Founders can also do other things like the first person to get the funding will get an extra 5% of the equity. Or in future, if someone's job becomes more important than we have pivoted, he or she will get 5%. Risk and hazards are the 'unknown unknown'. These are the stuff we know are going to happen but no one can guess about them. A certain amount of equity could also be set aside for the 'unknown unknown'.

### *Equity allocation and cliff investing*

Startups need employees to succeed, most businesses start in homes or garages individually and then people join. However, when allocating the equity most of the founders are in a zero-sum game. This can be a big mistake. Initially, a Startup needs motivated members that can stick with the Startup for the long term. Equity should be adequately given such that keep it keeps them motivated in long run. Also, a better way to deal with equity-based insecurities is to allocate through cliff investing. In cliff investing the partner will get its equity over a distributed period of time and will get nothing if fired within one year. The cliff vesting keeps the members motivated and at the same time, the other members can also feel relaxed that the equity will be given only if someone had contributed. It also helps avoid the deadlock if one of the co-founders decides to leave. The cliff vesting is discussed in more detail in the coming chapters.

## *The proposition method*

## Equity Distribution among confounders

### Development   Operations   Cash

| | Idea | Proto type | Design | Team | Activity | Management | Sales | Marketing | Operations | Accounting | |
|---|---|---|---|---|---|---|---|---|---|---|---|
| Person A | | | | | | | | | | | |
| Person B | | | | | | | | | | | |
| Person C | | | | | | | | | | | |
| Person D | | | | | | | | | | | |
| Person E | | | | | | | | | | | |

Founders can also divide the equity by measuring their corresponding value for Startup in terms of cash, sweat and intellectual property. Cash is quite easy to value in economic terms, however, it's hard to evaluate IP and sweat. The team can decide who did what. The figure shows the following proposition. It had three columns: development, operations and cash and in rows, different people who are involved. There are symbols at the intersection showing the person's status of contribution among the three topics. The big square, half straddle or a little square are in terms of what someone contributed to the business venture. Once entrepreneurs agree on this, they can then quantify, what each column is worth. Similarly, how much the idea is worth, can be quantified relative to somebody with customer fulfilment.

### 0.9 Survival with teams

*A people build A team while B people will make C teams. Build a team of intelligent people and make sure they work together.*

The chart shows the difference in the company survival (6 months to 24 months) given the different propositions of co-founders. The + and − signs are the positive and negative chances of surviving with time. When two co-founders invest the same amount of money, they increase the chances of staying together with the startup. The heterogeneous teams i.e., the team with different backgrounds has a low probability of staying together. The choices, the entrepreneurs make, can have an impact on the survival of the startup in surprising ways as per the research.

## Moving from individual to teams

|  | 6 months | 12 months | 10 months | 24 months |
|---|---|---|---|---|
| **Same Money Invested** | + | + | + | + |
| **Heterogenous Experience** | − | − |  |  |
| **Equal Split** | + | + | + | + |
| **Equal and Raised Round** | − | − | − | − |
| **Friends Before** |  |  |  |  |
| **Equal & Friends** | − |  |  |  |

An equal equity split has positive chances of staying together until the startup raises some amount of funding. When funding had not been raised, entrepreneurs do equal work and when they raise funding it's time to rethink everything (responsibility, roles and remuneration), which decreases the chance of staying together due to dissatisfaction and conflict. 'Friends first and equal equity split' is more likely to fall within six months. While surprisingly, uneven equity split is very common and around 47% of the companies have uneven equity split among founders.

*Uneven Equity Split: Gap in founder equity stakes*

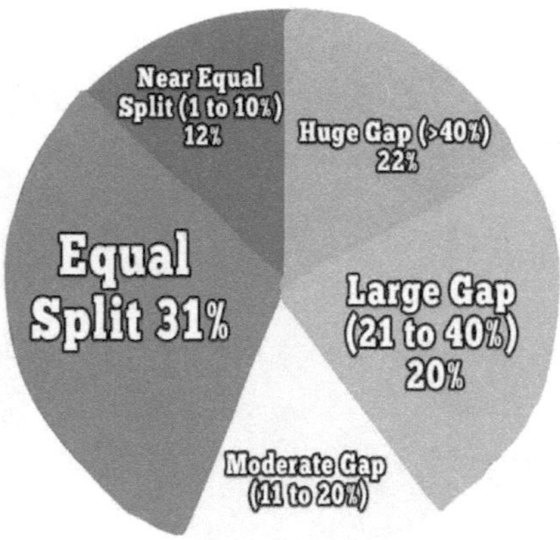

# 1. Sharpen your axe before you cut

### *1.1 Entrepreneurs are T-Shaped people*
*Embrace yourself, winter is coming! You are your business, got to develop the guts.*

**To become T shape, I have to join a gym, I am an oval**

Entrepreneurs are T-shaped people, meaning the depth of knowledge in one domain and breadth in other general areas. For example, strong footage and knowledge in Computer Science and breadth of knowledge in marketing, finance and HR. An author can say, what do I have to do with finance? But a book that doesn't sell is worthless! And then there is the question of having to figure out what the best price for the book is, not to mention how much profit I have made.

*Peeling onions*

Knowledge is compounded interest, each extra effort that you put into the project can pay rewards. If you are devoting eighty hours a week versus someone who is devoting forty hours a week, the amount of work done by someone in four years can be done by you in two years. Given the limited life expectancy of eighty years of which a major chunk goes to non-working time, it can make a big difference. There is a mantra that we had when we studied in college, which is to earn one crore. One crore rupee is needed for financial freedom. Financial freedom means when you earn 1 lakh rupees every month without doing any work and the 1 crore gives interest which fits the concepts. Also, compound interest was a very important concept. Let's say you have Rupees one crore and you are able to grow it at 20% CAGR for 35 years will become 1000 Cr.

## *1.2 Threshold Frequency*

There is a threshold to any work that we do. You want to learn to code, it's exciting for a couple of days, but things become ugly when the going gets tough. When we ship the rocket, we calculate what is the threshold frequency for the rocket to cross over to get beyond the gravitational force of the earth. Once the rocket reaches that point there is no need for fuel; it just sails smoothly. Anything that we choose to work on has some threshold. Once you cross the limit, a whole new world is waiting to be explored. Crossing the threshold is the most difficult part of all. To cross the threshold frequency, you need patience and perseverance. Those who learned to ride a two-wheeler, know the hardest part is to kick-start and maintain the balance in the initial few minutes. Once we are done, the motorcycle sails smoothly. When you sell your first product, you will realize the warmth of success. Use the spark to create a fire, and get into that comfort zone. The initial months of the Startup are the most painful.

We often think that startups have the highest number of failures. Think about becoming a superstar, a singer, a poet… people have given their whole lives trying hard to become one but may become just a cast member. The odds are everywhere, no matter which field you choose. There is a threshold in every field we choose. Once you reach the top, you will realise it is lonely there. How many people in a country of 130 crores can build a unicorn business? It is only a handful. Since you have this book in your hand, you too can make things happen.

***1.3 The Learning Curve***- Change the Boat, shift the learning curve

Back in the 17th century and before the invention of the refrigerator, icehouses were used to cool things. This was a stage where labours dug the ice and transported it to its destination. James Harrison, a Scottish Australian developed the first commercial ice-making machine in 1854. This was the second curve in a century where now the ice was produced. Initially, the industrial freezer was supplied to meat houses and breweries. In 1913, Fred Wolf developed the first residential freezer that consisted of an icebox on the top. This was the third phase where an industrial product was turned into a household product.

We all got to change the boat, change the learning curve, and develop new methods for ourselves when we saw no action or up-gradation in our existing systems. All we had was just a monotonous life. The ice changed the curve starting from manually transported by man to industrial use and then to personal consumables. The need is to get out of the comfort zone and that can pay a big reward. Each era had changed its form due to inventions in technology from icehouses to commercial refrigerator to residential use of freezers. Beyond jobs, you got to develop the system to change the curve that keeps you moving forward, write a book, start a business, make a documentary, develop a hardware-based product or the easiest of all is to learn to code and offer your service… this is the only way to get out of the loop. One should know when is the right time to change the boat. Changing the boat is important as after some time, the growth curve just flattens… like ten years in the same job, the learning, income and habits all get restricted.

## 1.4 Time management techniques don't work

*Don't manage time, manage your energy.*

- Most time management techniques you read about, don't work. The best way to kill time is to read a book on time management.

- The best way to manage time is to figure out what you can do best at that moment. Ask yourself, how much time you have; what you would like to do now; what you can complete best in this time. We are human beings and not robots and cannot be equally productive each morning. You need to figure out the best thing you can do during that time.

- Figuring out whether you are a morning person or an evening person also helps. Morning people wake up early and are focussed in the morning, while evening people are more focussed in the evening.

- Whether you are more productive at night or during the day, it is important to finish the toughest work in that time. Slay your demon in the morning/evening based on your productivity level, as time passes, the work gets bigger and bigger like demons and you can't finish it. Finishing the toughest work early will help maintain the pace and deep satisfaction of conquering the war even if your entire day wasn't very productive. As they say, if you win the morning, you win the day.

- Sometimes works grow big on you psychologically, and you choose not to do it. The trick is to force yourself or manipulate your mind by saying let's do it for five minutes and then another five minutes… once you force yourself for five minutes you will get into the rhythm. The same principle is the Pomodoro technique where your complete a task in chunks of 25 minutes. You do one job and then make a tomato on a paper or take a break for five minutes and do the second chunk and keep continuing.

- Figure out, two or three most important work of the day that you have to complete and this will fill up the whole day. Just plan for a few hours of important work, and your entire day will be filled up.

- ***Perfection is the biggest thief of time.***Let's assume you have completed 80% of work in an hour and to make the work perfect you took another two hours which is costly. In that time of two hours, to make the work perfect, you can complete some other work also. Let the work you have completed, pass on... don't be a perfectionist. Just do it and don't put a filter on it. Look at the first iPhone that Apple created... it was ugly! Some of your initial work will be ugly too.

- ***Don't invent things***to avoid work, procrastination is also the biggest thief of time. Ask yourself if you are inventing things to do, just in order to avoid work.

## *ADD IMAGE HERE*

- I compare work to dishwashing, the fewer dishes I have in the sink, the less I will be worried about them. The fewer things on your to-do list, the lesser reason you have to worry. I hate to think about the dirty laundry that had been kept for one week. Do yourself a favour and get it done first, it hardly takes one hour of work and it will free your mind, at least you will have two fewer things to bother about. Your mind will constantly demoralise whenever the work is in front of you or in memory.

- Keep the productive work separate from errands but errands can be costly sometimes and can't be ignored. Let's say you are about to write a book or notes and you don't have a pen; at least it will ruin a few hours for you. Club all the errands together… don't forget to buy pencils, vegetables and a notebook when you are returning from the office all at the same time in one go.

- Some are day creatures while some of us may be nocturnal. Some are mostly focussed during the morning. Make use of your focussed time to do the most important job of the day. Know in which zone you are and utilise your best time to get the maximum work done when you are in your comfort zone.

- Everybody has a cycle. When things go well your day is perfect; when you are not in the zone the whole day is missed, try to do at least one job when you are in the unproductive zone, this will build your rhythm slowly. It's okay to feel high and low; everybody does, its common but the key is to know when you are in the productive zone and how to utilise it best by removing the errands and at the same time, when you are not in much of a productive mood, how to remain focussed and keep moving?

- When it seems that you are not in the mood for working, just convince yourself to work for a few minutes and when you accomplish that, just trick your mind for a few more. If you do not touch the work, your mind will trick you and abstain you from doing the work altogether.

- Know how to juggle your work and maintain the pace of the same work throughout the day, switching between the works is not very productive. And often ask yourself if you are inventing things to avoid the work at hand.

- ***Become a master Juggler.*** People procrastinate and they do it often. Be a master juggler – throw a ball high in the sky so that it gives ample time to pick and throw the other ball in the sky. Founders take many parallel steps. Make sure you juggle the work and throw it so that it doesn't bother you at least for some time, pick something else, juggle and throw... repeat for a while and get a loop inside your system till you finish the work. Things will take their own course; things do not happen at your pace at your desired time and event but keep trying... sooner or later it will. It's okay if something doesn't kick off but it's not okay to lock yourself in a room and pressurise yourself. Everything works if you start working.

The best way to manage yourself is to not manage your time, but your energy. There are a whole lot of HBR articles on Managing Oneself by Peter F. Drucker. There is also wide self-help available like HBR's 10 Must Read on Managing Yourself (with the bonus article "How Will You Measure Your Life?" by Clayton M. Christensen). There are other resources like lectures. by Richard Hamming (1986); Randy Pausch's lecture on 'Time Management' and the video: 'Study Less Study Smart' by Marty Lobdell and 'How to Get More Done with a Lot Less Stress!' By Susan Lasky in ADDitude.

## *1.5 Taking Manageable steps*

Most entrepreneurs often jump and try to execute two ideas at a time. Bringing the existence of one idea is cumbersome… two ideas at the same time increase the odds! A person who paints a picture and tries to sell it, by opening a retail store are two different things. In the same way, writing a novel and printing in your own press are two businesses. The chances of survival increase if you focus on one thing. Opening a cattle farm and setting up a butcher shop will obviously divert the resources, energy and time which are limited initially. The way to do this is spilt when things get in shape. For example, a chain of restaurants doesn't start with 100 outlets, especially for those who are bootstrapping. Founders start with one, get everything fixed and running in one restaurant and then designate someone to open another outlet and then keep moving.

The other best way to launch a Startup is to take manageable steps one at a time. The project management technique gives a beautiful insight into the spiral framework. The spiral framework deals with finishing a subtask associated with launching, testing it and gathering feedback, if it works, then moving to the next subtask and keep repeating the loop, fixing the bottleneck. Launching and completing a massive task and eventually realising it's a failure, is waste of time and effort. The spiral as the word goes is like a subunit of a small task. The chances of rectifying the error if a mistake is made and solidifying the work and some of the benefits before moving ahead are important. Launching a bigger project and then rectifying things if an error is made can be cumbersome. The same approach is used in minimum viable products. There are hundreds of failures costing millions of dollars to companies when we plan to launch things at one go. .

### 1.6 Hunt like a tiger

If you want to be a high-performance Athlete, how good are you going to be if you always have deep scissor cuts on your body, if you are always twitching and running around and your limbs are completely out of control? In the same way, if you want to be effective in business, you need to have a clear, calm, cool collected mind. Warren Buffett goes walking in the sun. He doesn't sit around and constantly load his brain with nonstop information and folds his sleeve for every little thing.

Work like a tiger — you take a short sprint when hunting, hunt it down and then rest, and keep repeating the loop. Set small goals in that period. Even arranging your bed is a huge task… generate small achievements which will boost you. Bouncing is often difficult in tough times, but they don't last forever. Pick up the low-hanging fruits first, don't aim too high. There is a gem of wisdom by Naval Ravikant, JRE episode 1309.

## 1.7 Three Bucket principle

*Energy can neither be converted nor be destroyed, it can change from one form to another.*

Skills play a big role in the life of an entrepreneur. Entrepreneurs start with low cash, skill and ample time. The first bucket has the time, the second has the skill, and the third is capital which forms the basis of the 'three bucket principle'. When entrepreneurs start, the first two buckets drive to the third bucket. The second bucket (skill) plays a big role in the process of converting time into cash. The higher skilled you are, the better the chances of success and filling the third bucket. Also, initially, there is ample time that should be used to develop skills.

There are several graduates who had studied at IIT, in the non-computer science branch and had very limited career prospects. However, they chose to skill themselves in one area i.e., coding and made a fortune in Startups. The way to get all the colours in the world which is around ten million is just the three basic colours – Red, Green and

Blue (RGB). Often with the three attributes of time, skills and cash you can have the canvas of life beautifully painted.

If the second bucket is empty you are done… you are not in the game at all. Most startups struggle due to a lack of knowledge whether it is the skills of managing teams or the art of raising funds. Entrepreneurs should maintain due diligence to transact between the first bucket and the second one initially. The irony is that there is a trade-off between the three. As you pass through the Startup phases, the time will be limited and the cash will be pouring. Now, if you are skilled enough, you can delegate the work and can convert some of the cash into time. Often personal lives, if not balanced, destroys the professional career. There is a need to balance between the three resources time, cash and skill, considering what phase you are in, during the Startup process.

### 1.8 Three Kinds of people

Businesses are made by three kinds of people. First is highly skilled, second is people with lots of capital and third is people with a high network. The network is key to business trade and expansion, whether setting up an industry or pushing forward the project to get the letter of award. Being in touch with the right people can change the course to favour you.

The second kind of people belongs to the category who have capital. You want to put in 150 crores for setting up a steel processing unit, it's done! You don't have the skills, hire someone; you don't have the supply chain, build it.

The last category is the one in which 99.9% of the people belong. Some are skilled, some are not; while there is some, there is some hard work. If you can develop and design better products and services with analytical skills and find a gap in how the businesses are operating, and if you are smarter than the big companies and can outperform them, you are good to go. While a network can be built, money is difficult to make, and skills are comparatively easy to gather but with pain. Most people don't pass through the three phases. When you cross the threshold, you need them all for expansion.

## 1.9 A negatively skewed world view - Litigations are toxic

Litigation is the sport of kings. It is toxic for small entrepreneurs, and it should be avoided at all costs by Startups. Litigations are power plays that come down to money. Before it comes on the merit of judgement, money comes first. The worst settlement that founders can have are better than the litigations. There is no faster way to stop a Startup than by suing it. Big MNCs play the battle on the ground with the small fish by just suing them when they stand in their way.

When someone sues a Startup all the money and focus will go to the lawyer and the litigation, not the firm. It's a strategy technology companies use. It is a small world. There is an excellent documentary *Print the Legend* by Luis Lopez and J. Clay Tweel which just highlights the journey of two entrepreneurs and the battle with one big company, Stratasys. Stratasys, MakerBot and Formlabs are all in the business of 3D printing which obviously makes them compete with each other. How litigations are used to take the counterpart out of the competition, is crafted beautifully in the documentary.

## 1.10 Biases to watch out for!

*Make sure you squeeze every ounce available for a perfect start.*

**This is a machine that squeeze the biases out of minds.**

Cognitive biases are common among entrepreneurs. Scientifically, to counter the bias we use the term 'epistemology' – *How you know what you know*. Epistemology questions the knowledge and the existing belief. It is often important to ask this question to remove the biases. Entrepreneurs often start solo, and understanding all sorts of cognitive biases may help in the long run and make better decisions.

*Planning fallacy: Failing to plan is planning to fail*
We tend to overestimate the benefits of the task and underestimate the duration it will take. In most cases, it takes thrice as much time for the entrepreneurs to deliver something, as the time they decide to deliver the work. Therefore, try to allot yourself double the time that you think any task will take. The estimation of time if missed

can delay product prototyping, shipping or development. The Kickstarter launched products is a good example where it's normal to get the work delayed by a period, from six months to one year.

*Confirmation Bias*

Confirmation deals with the tendency to remember the information that validates our idea rather than those that reject our beliefs. The attributes that are appreciated well by customers stick to us while the negative review is ignored. Evaluating the negative review in a logical and analytical way is often important, rather than just reinforcing the existing belief. The false consensus effect is similar to confirmation bias which deals with the tendency to overestimate people's agreement with their beliefs and values. It makes people overvalue their opinion and incorrectly think that everybody is agreeing with him.

*Hindsight Bias*

The hindsight bias is the tendency to see random events, as more predictable and correlate it with the cognitive insight as the "I knew it" approach. Investors also fall into a trap and feel they could have predicted which companies would have become more successful. This bias occurs due to the ability to view the events as inevitable and validate the existing notion even if we misremember the information.

*The anchoring biases*

In an era of social media, people always feed their brains with constant information. In the absence of any information available, people generally consider the notion that they encounter first. We tend to be influenced by the first piece of information, it's a phenomenon referred to as the anchoring bias or anchoring effect.

*Sunk Cost Fallacy*

We often tend to value more when we have invested time and money. We as humans are averse to losses when we are leading them. Entrepreneurs should not consider the sunk cost when taking a managerial decision. This bias is predatory as we tend to work more on the projects even after getting feedback of no success, as we have devoted enough amount of time and resources to the project.

# 2. STARTistics

*Application of Statistics to startups and weird facts from the statistical lenses*

Statistics is nothing but the science of drawing a conclusion from data. It is the study of the law of chances which has historically been used only for one thing in the past i.e., gambling. Statistics are everywhere and drawing conclusions is important whether it is manufacturing, quality control, clinical testing, environmental monitoring, polling, racial bias, or the law. The data is the raw material for statisticians.

A statistician's work is like detective work. We are a negative people because we keep rejecting the null. We may have a different worldview of seeing things in terms of how far the standard deviation is, and whether P values[1] less than .05 or not. The world is skewed for us negatively or positively, which we try to make perfectly normal. You can see the delight on the face of a person when finding normally distributed data points, and we try to search for normality[2] in everything to apply the empirical rule[3]. We see an estimator as biased and we always try to find the best-unbiased estimator. Statistics deals with numbers, and numbers don't lie. As Benjamin Disraeli said, "There are three kinds of lies: lies, damned lies, and statistics." If it's easy to lie with numbers, then it's easier to lie without them. This chapter draws the philosophy from some of the statistical concepts we use commonly.

## [1] **P Value**

1. We used a CI to test our hypothesis. Another approach is with P-Values! P-value (short for probability value) is the probability of obtaining data as or more extreme than the data we actually observed, assuming the null hypothesis is true. It tells us how consistent the observed data are with the null hypothesis. P-values range from 0 to 1, inclusive. A small p-value indicates the observed data and null hypothesis are inconsistent, while a large p-values indicates that they are consistent.

2. It gives the measure of the credibility of the null hypothesis. Small p-values give evidence against

the null. The probability that if you did the experiment again and the null hypothesis were true, that you observe a value of the test statistic as extreme as the one you saw the first time.

3.  It picks up the repeatability idea. If something is true (i.e., the null hypothesis) then you should be able to replicate the observed results. A small p − values says that it would be hard to replicate, hence the small p-values offers evidence against the null.

4.  We reject the Null hypothesis when the P Value is small, usually defined as smaller than $\alpha=0.05$ . The mnemonic we use is "If P is low Null must go!" We use software programs (typically) to calculate p-vales. P values are very common in scientific articles

After running experiments one of the statistics that we check to reject the null is P Value. P value is a probability statement which answers, if the null hypothesis were true what is the chance of observing the same statistic as in the current experiment? Less p value simple means that the same statistics have very low probability of getting the same result if we replicate the same and we reject the null hypothesis that says that there is no difference between the expected an observed result.

## [2] The Normal Distribution

This is the most ubiquitous of all statistical distribution. It is often known as Bell Curve. Many statistical techniques require the assumption of Normality. It is characterized by the mean and standard deviation. If you know these two features, then you know everything.

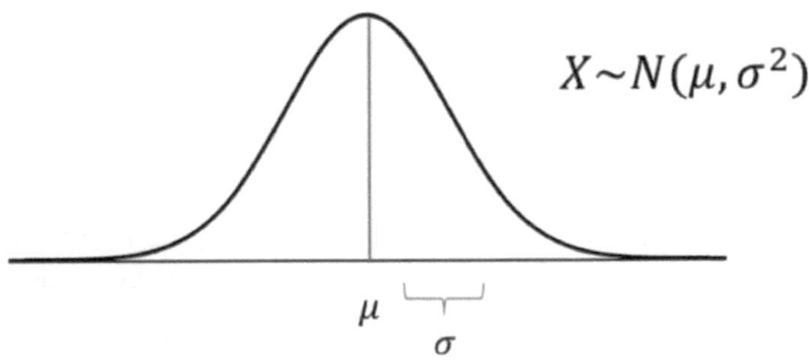



If we calculate sample mean repeatedly from the sample of sample size from the same population then we have a distribution that is mound-shaped, symmetric and centered near the mean.

The normal distribution is a theoretical model of a distribution. We don't expect any particular distribution in reality to fit this distribution exactly, but often distributions may fit quietly. We denote the normal distribution as $X \sim N$ $(\mu, \sigma^2)$. We read it as X is distributed normally with mean $\mu$, and standard deviation, $\sigma^2$.

The normal distribution is centered on $\mu$, and standard deviation $\sigma^2$. The shape of the normal distribution is mound shape and symmetric. But the distribution model comes in many forms depending upon the mean and standard deviation. Large value of σ result in flat, spread-out normal distribution while smaller value of σ lead to peaked narrow distribution.

### ³ **The Empirical Rule**

If the data is bell shaped and symmetric then we say it is approximately normal. The mean and standard deviation summarize the data efficiently in these circumstances. The **EMPIRICLE RULE**only applies when the data is approximately normal.

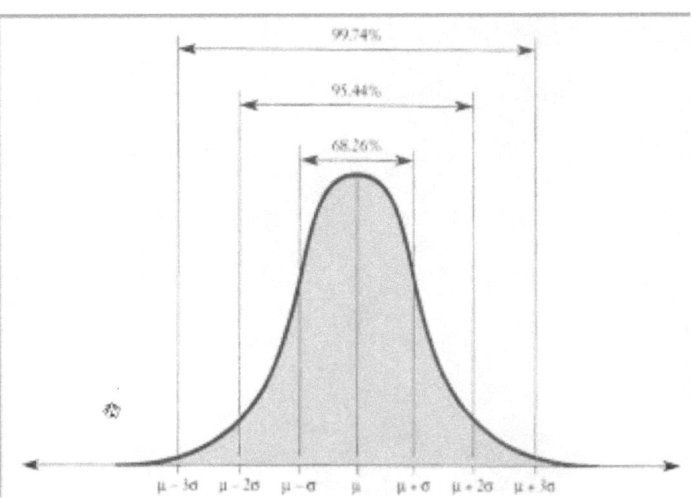


Empirical rule provides a rule of thumb for normal data — it ties together the mean and standard deviation, into a rule that establishes where most of the data should lie. If the data is outside this range, then it is an atypical observation. The rule says that:

- 68% of the data is within 1 standard deviation of the mean.

- 95% of the data is within the 2-standard deviation of the mean.

- Essentiality all (99.7%) of the data is with in the 3-standard deviation of the mean.

## 2.1 Conditional Expectation

The expectation is the mean or average, while [1]conditional expectation is a better measure than expectation and is used when receiving extra information. The conditional expectation incorporates the information available prior to the occurrence of the final event. In other words, we say, given that an event 'A' had already occurred, what the probability of getting an event B is. For example, if we rolled a dice and got a 5, what is the probability that when we roll the dice again the sum of both would be a 10? The sample space also gets reduced to get the conditional probability. The principle of the spiral framework in project management is widely known, which relies heavily on the concept that instead of building and testing massive projects, we undertake small projects that are standalone and we keep building the loop of smaller projects to get a complete set of projects.

The conditional expectation is just a synonym for a spiral framework rather than working on a single big project.

Concepts like MVP applies the same. Instead of building the product at one go with hundreds of features the principles, just focus on the bare minimum that is the core offering. Then launch it, test it and reiterate it. If it doesn't look ugly when you have launched the first version of the product, then you are late to launch, even the most famous brands like Google and Apple looked ugly when they were launched. One of the important aspects of building a great product is to build a feedback loop, incorporate the finding, and test and fix the flaws that you found in the first versions. This is exactly what conditional expectation does. I Incorporate the prior information and rebuild the probability on the basis of the information, to give an accurate picture of what had already happened.

## 4 <u>Conditional Probability</u>

Conditional probability is a measure of the probability of an event occurring given that B has happened what is the probability of happening A. If the child is malnourished, what is the probability that it will have disease? Given that the moisture content in air is high, what is the probability that it will rain?

$$P(A|B) = \frac{P(A \cap B)}{P(B)}$$

## 2.2 Uncertainty

Entrepreneurs are a rare species that love to live in their own dreams and make things happen that the world can aspire to… like Steve Jobs and Apple. They also face uncertainty. Dealing with uncertainty and ambiguity is one of the Herculean tasks that if handled properly could be a great deal. Uncertainty can be dealt with [2]Probability. Entrepreneurship is more about dealing with tolerance, ambiguity and uncertainty. All the pain that entrepreneurs go through, whether it is living like a mouse in a church tunnel or saving the bucks on laundry will be worthless when you are not able to execute and rectify the holes in the Startup. When the stakes are high, no one wants to end with no returns at the end of the year of the start-up phase. It's the dream of getting into IPO rather than handing over your brainchild to a stepdad CEO in lieu of big money or just failing. The task of an entrepreneur is to develop better solutions than the existing ones through wiser decisions. If you want to build a unicorn, you have got to solve a billion problems.

## [5] **Probability**

Probability is important as it helps in answer to the question that research might pose. For example: Will a clinical test gives wrong result? What are the chances of having a break failure during a long drive? Given that its winter season, what is the chances of raining? Probability is a measure of uncertainty or how likely is an event to occur?

## 2.3 *What central limit theorem teaches us?*

*Look for the long run.*

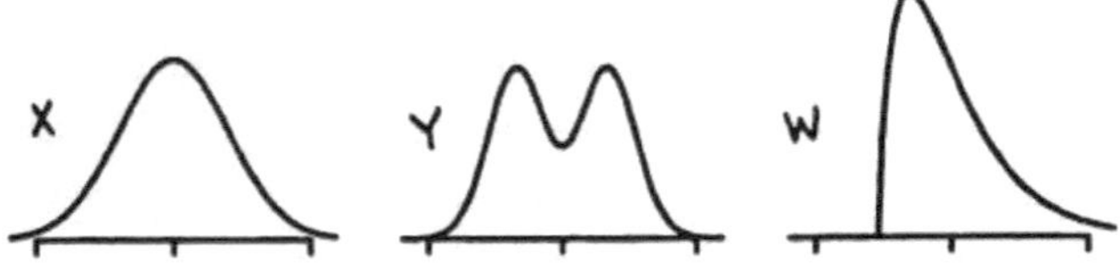


Life is full of ups and downs if you look it up in a short span of time. Incidents happen, some bad and some good. While the bad incidents affect most rather than the good ones. Negative thought stays for a long time and keeps you worrying. But the moment you turn the negative thoughts into positive ones, they will fly. No matter how many bad incidents or events or skewed data we have, life in the long term is always normal.

No matter how much the data is skewed the mean of the data will always be normal. If one takes a random sample of size n from a population and then as n gets a large mean of the distribution, approaches the normal distribution. In other words, it says regardless of the shape of the original distribution the average result is normal. Similarly, we can take samples of incidents to gauge our life accomplishments and failures, and when the sample size increases, the CLT[3] kicks in and the views are just normalised. If we pick a few skewed incidents and then measure them they must not be normal.

## [6] **Central Limit Theorem**

The CLT states that if random samples of size n are drawn repeatedly from any population with mean μ variance $\sigma^2$, then when n is relatively large (n>= 30 for most distribution) the distribution of these sample means will be approximately normal. In layman terms, by repeatedly and randomly drawing sample averages from any population, we can create a new distribution that we know will be normal.

$$\bar{x} \sim N\left(\mu, \frac{\sigma^2}{n}\right) \quad \text{Note: } \frac{\sigma}{\sqrt{n}} \text{ is called the "standard error of the mean"}$$

The Distribution of sample means of size n drawn from the same population is centered around μ and has a variance of $\sigma^2/n$. The distribution of the sample means is symmetric and mound shaped (i.e. Normal distribution). Take any population, no matter its distribution!

The CLT just touches the philosophical side of humans. Things always move in a zigzag motion, sometimes up and sometimes down; we fail and we succeed, in some extreme cases it can happen to be multiple failures and then success, or vice versa. Look at the movement of stocks, the heart monitor always goes 0 to 1 or 1 to 0. Life is exactly the same aspect or phenomenon.

While monitoring the day-to-day events, we sometimes fail and sometimes succeed; sometimes we achieve it, and sometimes we completely miss it, but that is okay. Even if we fail half of the time in these events, we would achieve our goals significantly. CLT is just an altered version of that, no matter how things are distributed in short term, in long term it is always distributed normally; the things are the long run always looks normal, so you don't need to get disappointed. Just relax about the fact that it is normal and in the long term, things will be very significantly accumulated.

## 2.4 Correlation

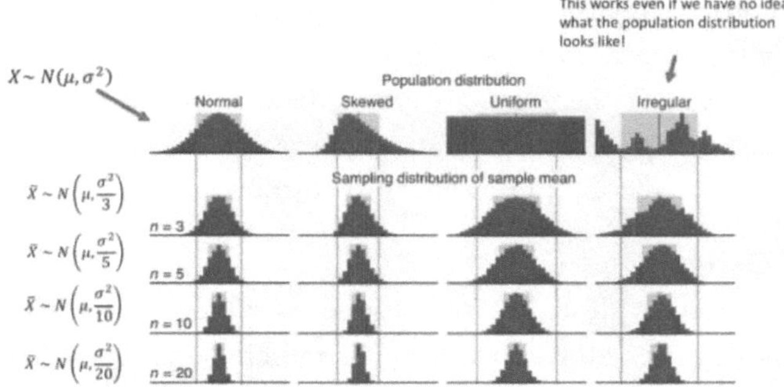


- Through CLT, we can make inferences about the world around us from relatively small, random samples of target population

- By using rather, a sample data, we can make inferences rather than simply describing the data we have at hand.

Correlation[7] measures the strength of linear association and it's a unitless quantity. Two variables can be correlated, but may not have a causal relationship in statistics we say 'correlation does not imply causation'. Correlation helps us correlate our offering with the users, the more the users like what we offer, the better the prospects of making a million dollars in the game. Whether you talk about features, sales, operations, or production, everything needs to incline with the customers, things have to be correlated with the user, whether we craft pricing, launch, scale, or offering, at the centre the user had to be simulated. The more things are correlated and within the limit the better shape we will be in. The organization should be customer-centric. The product has to be user-centric not the founder or idea-centric. At the core of the offering, there have to be users. If there are no users, then obviously, we don't need that product. This can only be achieved by correlating the idea, actions and business to customers.

## 7 **Correlation**

Correlation describes the degree to which two variables move in coordination with one another. When the value of two variables tend to increase (or decrease) together, we say that we have a **positive linear relationship**. We say the relationship is linear, when the observation lies in a straight line. When the value of one variable increase while the other decreases, we say that is negative linear relationship or negative correlation.

Correlation coefficient $\varrho$ , gives the numerical summary of the strength and direction of linear relationship between two quantitative variables. It will always be between -1 and +1. 1 or -1 means perfect liner association. The sign indicates the direction of relationship.

A study may show a strong correlation between two variables. For example, the number of deaths in a given year or number of kites flying in the sky. **Correlation does not imply causation**. Causal inferences can only be drawn in randomised control trials. We randomly assign groups to treatment or control group and control the various other confounding variables.

## **Covariance**

Covariance does not give the strength of linear relationship, only the sign or direction. We can just gauze the relationship. We standardise the covariance by dividing it with their standard deviation. That is called **Correlation**!

$$r_{xy} = s_{xy} / s_x s_y$$

$s_{xy}$ is the sample covariance of x and y, and sx,sy are sample standard deviation of x and y. Covariance is similar to correlation, but retains the scale of the data? Covariance appears in the variance of the linear combination of random variable.

## 2.5 Confidence Interval

*Not sure, but somewhere close!*

Confidence Interval[8] helps us define how much we can absorb the shock of deviation when targeting an aim, hence it becomes an important value to consider. We can't expect to miss the deadline daily and achieve the goal. But we can have a slight deviation from the normal routine and a couple of failures and achieve the goal. Whenever targeting any goal, quantify it, and put a CI on it; the bands will help you decide whether it is Okay and whether we doing good so far. If not, what is the deviation and what measures can be taken to correct it?

Always ask for confidence intervals in real-life business or assumptions. If the confidence interval is wide, the result can be very misleading for someone who has just started his journey.

Precision is important no matter what you do. Specifically, when raising funds, hiring employees, and developing products, CI are helpful. If you are most of the time beyond the CI it is expected that you will not meet your goals.

## [8] **Confidence Interval**

A point estimate is a single number. A confidence interval provides additional information about variability. Confidence interval gives the probability or range of estimates that an unknown parameter will falls between a pair of values. Using the concept of the standard error (SE), we can create a confidence interval: Point estimate $\mp$ 2 x SE

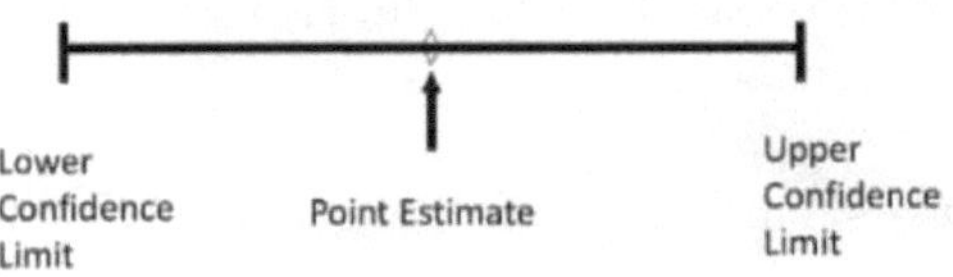


The standard error represents the standard deviation with the estimate, and roughly 95% of the time the estimate will be within 2 standard errors of the parameters. When we say we have 95% confidence that our interval contains the true population mean, formally, what we mean is that "95% of samples of this size will produce confidence intervals that capture the true population parameter." This is correct but a little long winded, so we sometimes say "we are 95% confident that the true parameter lies in our interval.

## 2.6 Leverage Data Points

*The secrets to driving the business*

Statisticians love leveraged data points, they have the potential to drive a whole regression[6] line or model. They change our results drastically. We live in an age of leverage. This means that our actions can be multiplied by a thousand-fold. Some things have high leverage like either podcast or writing a piece of code., While some have no leverage, like setting up factories and industries that are capital and labour intensive. Even you can leverage your actions by making people work for you. This hugely impacts good decision-making. The good decision impact can now be multiplied a thousand times by just switching the key of leverage and you can influence thousands and millions of people. Certainly, it also leads to a better outcome.

The news of making businesses is just a click. Write machine algorithms, make computers smarter, and write some codes. Just digitise everything… food, relationships we build, all this is the way to leverage. Web-based applications have leverage because one person can write while the whole world uses them. Also, the marginal cost of producing the service is less and is close to nothing.

To be honest, if we talk about leverage, we can say, it is the minimum input that produces the maximum output. Digital, technological, and media are leveraged industries with a huge amount of output that can be produced with minimum input. You can write one piece of code for the whole world but it's not applicable in other fields. It is like you can't produce one piece of bread for the whole world to eat from the same resources that are required in the production of that one piece of bread. In the same way, media is also leveraged. One great channel or couple of good videos can be watched by thousands of people and can subsequently be converted into profits. And entrepreneurs should always be on the lookout for leverage.

## 9 <u>**Simple Linear Regression**</u>

We will create a model that predicts temperature as a linear function of cricket chirp rate

**Dolbear Law:**Amos Dolbear claimed in 1897 that there is a relationship between crickets chirping and temperature. The higher the temperature, the faster the chirping! It raised the two fundamental questions. How can we describe temperature changes given the number of cricket chirps? Can we use chirping to predict temperature? The answer is yes using simple linear regression.

He concluded that cricket chirps can be used to predict the temperature. The more cricket chirps per minute, the higher the expected average temperature. The whole experiment gave the genesis of SLR which was in shape of lines plotted against dots which was the observed data.

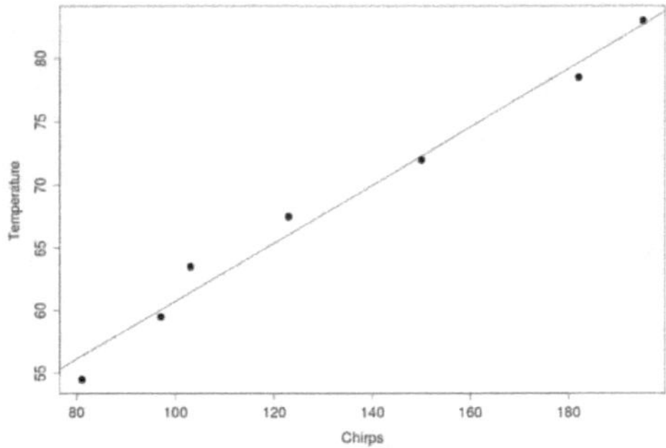

SLR is a method for fitting a line to scatterplot of data. The line can be viewed as the best line for the purpose of describing and predicting a quantitative variable with an outcome. It gives us an estimated mean of the outcome for each value of our predictor variable.

A linear **model predicts** a response variable, y, using a linear function of explanatory variables. **Simple linear regression predicts** on response variable, y, as a linear function of one explanatory variable, x.

## 2.7 Outliers

*The perfect dot that will drag all the profits*

Statisticians always plot the residuals and are on the lookout for outliers. Whether an outlier is good or not, is completely dependent on perspective. Entrepreneurs should after a certain stage, focus on outliers during the initial phase. Like the 80:20 principle, according to which 20% of customers generate 80% of the revenue. These are the coders who have the capability to outperform the rest of the team by 20 times. They can easily decide which of the product features are used mostly by our customers and which are redundant pieces. Or, which are the products or services that are generating more revenue and consuming fewer resources. While the revenue-consuming products should be discarded, the same is true for Apple and Macintosh. Just spotting the outliers by plotting a picture can help gain a better insight, whether in terms of restricting the company or getting a roadmap ahead.

## 2.8 Interpolation is good extrapolation is bad

*Assumptions on assumptions can be delusional.*

There are two words that we use in statistics — interpolation and extrapolation. Interpolation is good while extrapolation is bad. Statisticians always remain cautious when extrapolating outside the range of data, because we have no data to validate the estimate. When starting the business, we should interpolate not extrapolate. In other words, we should choose our existing domain, and expertise when starting up. Startups in completely different unrelated fields are extrapolation which is bad. It's good for a person who is serving the industry for decades to start a bakery business, rather than exploring a completely different field. The most successful entrepreneurs are those people who created their Startup with something in which their expertise already existed, like, in the case of Flipkart, the founders work in Amazon, for Snapdeal, the founders worked in Microsoft.

*Steve Jobs* in his famous speech delivered at the *University of Michigan* spoke about how early life skills connected the dots backwards. But make sure you also connect the dots forward. It is the foresightedness of an entrepreneur, a small light at the end of the tunnel which motivates him to accomplish his journey. If you can't learn from your past mistakes you are doomed to fail to understand, how you take the dot forward. To be honest, you need to connect the dot both ways… both forward and backwards. The first one will make you take decisions based on minute details and expertise gathered from connecting backwards; while the second will align the company's vision and mission that will motivate you to move forward.

## Degree of freedom

The higher the degree of freedom entrepreneurs have, the more the control and flexibility in running the Startup. The constraints are the angels/VC, technological support, outsourced work, etc. The degree of freedom is one of the important concepts. Let's say we have an outside investor; he can impose restrictions.

In statistical terms, the degree of freedom is calculated as the difference between two quantities. The sample size n and the number of other sample statistics (like variance, Standard deviation mean or others) are used in the calculation of sample statistics. The degree of freedom of the sample mean is n, as no other sample statistics are used in the final calculation of the sample mean. The degree of freedom of sample variance[7] is n-1 as the sample mean, $\bar{x}$ is used in calculating the sample variance. Please check the formula of variance, there is a mean included in it.

Another way to think of the degree of freedom is in terms of constraints on the possible values of observation. Suppose we have three numbers x1, x2 and x3 and we have no constraints… then each number could be anything. Bust now suppose we say $\bar{x}=3$. So, you can choose any two values and the third value is constrained by the sample mean. When x1=1 and x2=3 then x3 must be 5 when $\bar{x}=3$.

## 7 <u>Variance</u>

To calculate the variability, we measure the distance of each observation from the mean. After measuring the distance of each observation, we square the distance to make it non negative so that they don't cancel each other. The final number is called variance. In other words, variance is the average of square distance or deviation from the sample mean.

$$S^2 = \frac{(x_1 - \bar{x})^2 + (x_2 - \bar{x})^2 + \cdots (x_n - \bar{x})^2}{n}$$

The variance is expressed in unit squared. For example, if, our data is in meters the variance is in meter square. To return to meters we take square root. When we take square root, it is called standard deviation.

Observations: 3,6,4,7,1,3

| $x_i$ | $(x_i - \bar{x})$ | $(x_i - \bar{x})^2$ |
|---|---|---|
| 3 | -1 | 1 |
| 6 | 2 | 4 |
| 4 | 0 | 0 |
| 7 | 3 | 9 |
| 1 | -3 | 9 |
| 3 | -1 | 1 |
| $\sum x_i = 24$ | 0 | $\sum (x_i - \bar{x})^2 = 24$ |

So $n = 6$. $\bar{x} = 4$. $s^2 = 4.8$. $s = 2.191$.

## Standard deviation

The *standard deviation* for a quantitative variable measures the spread of the data. It gives us convenient single number summary of variability or dispersion among a set of observation. The standard deviation gives a rough estimate of the typical distance of a data value from the mean. The larger the standard deviation, the more variability there is in the data and the more spread out the data are.

# 3. Innovation

## *3.1 Collecting Ideas*

*Ideas are gems, collect them, refine them and execute them.*

Two Way Decision Table

|  | **No Fire** | **Fire** |
|---|---|---|
| *No Alarm* | No Error | Type II |
| *Alarm* | Type I | No Error |

The null hypothesis is a condition of no fire while the alternative hypothesis is fire. The alarm corresponds to the rejection of the null hypothesis.

|  | **Ho** | **Ha** |
|---|---|---|
| *Accept Ho* | No Error | Type II |
| *Reject Ho* | Type I | No Error |

- The idea is a seed. We plant it, water it and protect it, and it grows into a tree, giving us fruits and shade. The same is true for business ideas.

- We often face a stressful time when ideas just pop up every second for a couple of minutes. This is the time when we give birth to ideas in a bunch; it is a crucial period, note down every idea that you get because they are perishable, and you can ponder upon them later.

- An idea is worthless until it gets executed. That's why people say it's better to bet on a jockey than a horse. Startups are less about the idea and more about the execution. We made the idea work layer by layer, just like a house is made brick by brick by an architect.

## *Selecting an idea:*

- Entrepreneurs often struggle to find the idea to start a business. The key to getting into the meat is to reduce it to its bare essence. Paul Hawken suggests, that an idea should arise from deep within you, it should be solely yours and cannot be copied or stolen. It should be unique to you. It's like painting a picture or writing a novel and they are clear, concise and free of clutter.

- The other way to choose a better idea is to ask what problem you are trying to solve. It will help stay focussed and get to the root of the problem.

- Another way to judge which idea is better is to choose the idea that sticks with you for a long time.

- Next-gen products are not just produced in factories but are also cheap, and do not cost harm to the environment. We are just making better products. We don't only need successful products but also sustainable ones that consume less energy, water and raw material. When selecting the idea have the vision of sustainability in mind.

- *Error in selecting an idea:*Statisticians deal with two types of error, type 1 error[1], which is executing the innocent person and type 2 error is to free the guilty person. When selecting ideas there is a chance of these two types of errors. When an idea you have is good and you reject it, it is a type 1 error; or everything is wrong with the idea and still, you select it is a type 2 error. When you select a wrong idea, you get a chance to work on it which costs time and resources and will eventually be proven false otherwise. While in the first case, the idea never gets an opportunity to see the light of day.

- **Shortlisting Idea:**A better way to shortlist an idea from a bunch of ideas is by practically testing it for the actual customers. Often ideas are in raw shape and do not have a soul in them, the way to give them identity is to name the startup, and write down the online description and problem description of the Startup. Further, the entrepreneur could build a logo and prepare a website and domain name for all the ideas that they have in mind. Ideally, three ideas are good to test and compare. After finalising and giving a shape of the bubble/idea it is not ready to get tested. An online campaign can be used using Facebook, Instagram or Google to check which idea performs better than the rest. You can measure attributes like CTR, CPC, and CPA to evaluate the success of one idea among others. These attributes can be easily gathered during the online campaign and can be compared.

## 11 <u>__Type 1 and Type 2 Error__</u>

- Alpha Error (Type I): Rejecting H0 when it is true.

- Beta Error (Type II): Failing to reject H0 when it is False.

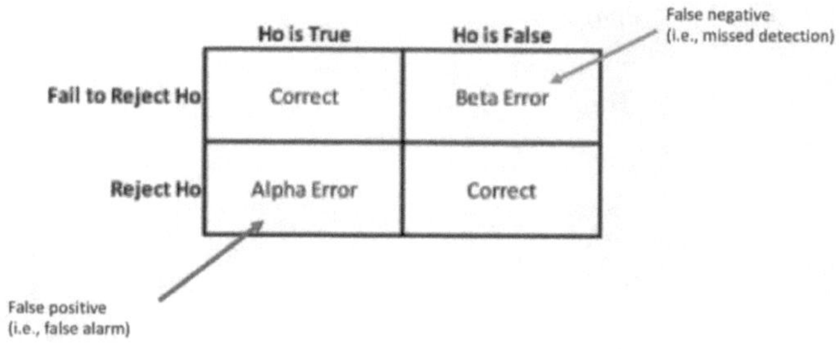

# Two Mnemonics for Type I and Type II Errors

## False Vs. Missed Detection:

- Type I Error: "False Alarm" (10 letters)

- Type II Error: "Missed Detection" (15 letters)

- 15 letters > 10 letters, just as II > I

## False Positive vs. False Negative:

- Type I Error: "I" has one vertical line, just like "p".

- Thus, a Type I error is associated with a false positive.

- Thus, II Error: "II" has two vertical lines, just like "n".

- Thus, a Type II error is associated with false negative.

- $H_0 = Innocence$

- $H_a =$ Guilt

$H_0 =$ Innocence
$H_a =$ Guilt

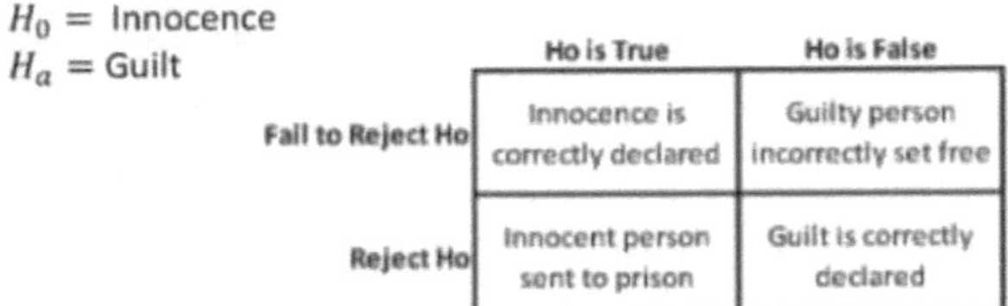

|  | Ho is True | Ho is False |
|---|---|---|
| Fail to Reject Ho | Innocence is correctly declared | Guilty person incorrectly set free |
| Reject Ho | Innocent person sent to prison | Guilt is correctly declared |

### 3.2 Solving the big problems

*For some problems are headaches, but for some others, they are tools to make money!*

We all solve problems – some small, some big. Solving gives immense satisfaction. Some of us manage to change the lives of people by solving their needs, and some of us are good at fixing the handle of a knife lying in the kitchen. The intensity of satisfaction is the same whether we solve a small problem or big, while the change that it brings to the world had wide differences. My uncle feels quite satisfied when roping a bench or driving a nail in the wall while others are busy finding what to solve.

Some problems are like a single shot, nail it and leave it, some problems required constant intervention while others are like a project sheet, until and unless you don't complete each and every detail related to the project, the problems don't solve. After solving the problem gives us continuous work and we brew the benefit once all the resources are channelized.

A problem can be plotted against the time required to solve it, the skills required and constant intervention. The task that requires more time, needs constant intervention, and high skills are the big ones that create huge amount of cash like Tesla and spaces X. When we plot the diagram, as we move closer to the bottom the reward of solving the problem may be limited to a few people and may not even be monetarily rewarded.

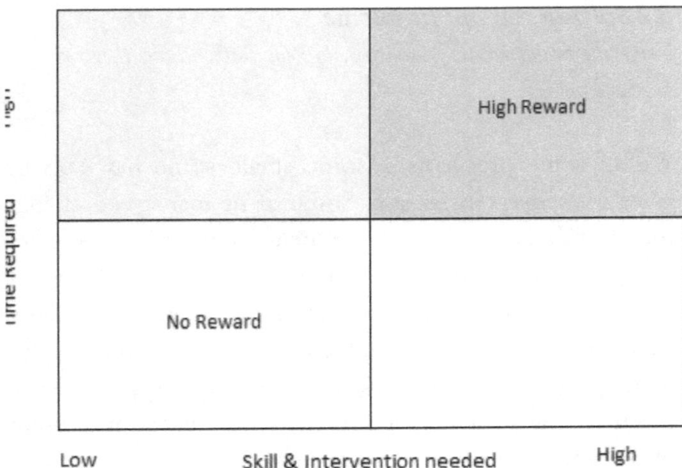


The x+ and y+ are the sweet spots for a problem that needed a good effort and are wise to consider while x-ve and Y + are also good to look for. While the rest of the two quadrants should be outsourced like the four-hour work week author did. The high income and skill category are worth targeting.

### *3.3 Different ways to Innovate*

*Innovation is just a weapon for optimization!*

### *Build it they will come*

This approach is an engineering-dominated approach, founders skip the customer feedback and demand validation. It follows the principle of a leap of faith, the focus is entirely on product development and turning their vision into reality. Taking a deep dive could be good sometimes, however, it may be an excuse for an entrepreneur who is timid and did not want to get out of the building to validate his assumptions. This approach is risky and without a proper feedback loop, it is often difficult, entrepreneurs often develop a product that nobody cares about.

*Waterfall planning*

Work is completed in a sequential approach; the effort is to move to the next stage which happens when the first stage passes the test. We divide the process into different phases, design, code and test. Entrepreneur further moves on, only when they pass a formal review. The following stages can be part of waterfall planning concept exploration, business plan formation, target segment, product design and development, testing and alpha launch. The sequential step to launch a product also has a drawback, as following something rigidly and stepwise can also block the other work. Sometimes a parallel approach is needed to consider rather than stepwise refinement.

**Being first with the most strategy:**One of the ways to be innovative is 'being first with the most strategy' which implies you will be the first one to execute the concepts. The atom bomb, the radar lab, the proximity fuse, and then putting a man on the Moon were all innovative efforts which used the 'first with the most strategy'. They need ambitious aim and disruptive thinking, however, the odds of failure associated with this approach are often high.

This strategy is very much like a moon shot, a deviation of a fraction to the arc or crash landing will destroy the mission and the missile disappears into outer space. This is no scope to adjust or correct. It's like an old Swiss story of Wilhelm Tell, the archer, whom the tyrant promised to pardon if he succeeded in shooting an apple off his son's head on the first try. If he failed, he would either kill the child or be killed himself. There can be no almost-success or near-miss. There is only success or failure. This strategy requires an enormous amount of will, resources and teamwork.

## *Just do it!*

This approach is also based on the aspiration of the entrepreneur but without a development blueprint. There is also a need for strong initial guidance to pass through the process in one go. This process also relies on feedback from various stakeholders. While it's difficult to say which of the methods is best, a combination of a few methods depending upon the stage of the Startup could be beneficial.

## *3.4 Replicative vs Innovative*

### *Innovation is the key to success*

Innovation has many forms, which are often misused or underrepresented. Replicative entrepreneurship is a much better way than innovative entrepreneurship for the masses, not everyone can be Sergey Brin, Larry Page or Steve Jobs. Peter Theil in his book 'Zero to One' explains the process of creating an innovative offering. In most cases taking something forward from 'One' onward is a better proposition rather than creating a true invention which starts at step 'Zero'. For example, in India, instead of coming up with a new story in movies, Indian producers are replicating the same movie. Movies that are successful in the southern part of India, are replicated to give a better result at the same time STARisk is minimal because they already have the response of the audience in one part of India. The model had been successful whether we talk about movies or companies. There are a plethora of companies in India and china like Flipkart, Baidu, Xiaomi,

PVR, and CCD, which started just as a replica of their foreign counterparts. Asian companies have been known for creating replicas of proven products, brands and business models, especially from the USA and adapting them for the local market with a tweak.

Baidu is the Google of China; Alibaba is eBay and Xiaomi is Apple. Innovation in many ways is a luxury of profitable companies. As an entrepreneur you may not be profitable, you may not have the capabilities to start at step 'Zero' because when you start you start solo. To be successful you don't need to start something new and noble, but you may need to tweak it to meet the need of the market you are catering to. We often focus more on innovation towards products and services but forget about market innovation. Bringing something new from one geography to another often gives the same perk as its counterpart. There is plenty of money to make traditionally in a bank, finance, retail stores, food and beverage stores, tax services, clothing manufacturers, and chemical companies.

New or product-based innovation is like we are hitting a peak, so new and noble means it is untried and untested in the market. If the objective is financial gain, there is plenty of room to make money the old-fashioned way i.e., by creating a replica. There are plenty of people who made money in traditional ways, like packaging chemical products for companies, and insurance, where the banks were kept open from 9, am to 5 pm, instead of 9 am to 3 pm. Many started a candle company. An investor once asked if the candle industry is in continuous decline for the past 800 years, what makes you think it's a growing industry? It turns out he created a multibillion-dollar company aggregating candle companies. So, think hard about the definition of entrepreneurship that you want to model, it has not been necessary new and noble in terms of product or service.

# 4. Business Model

*Ever wondered whether to disclose your business model or not and what the pillars of the business model are and why it is on hype?*

## *4.1 The Foundation of model*

The attribute that differentiates a well-established company from a Startup is the business model. Established companies have a leakproof business model while the business model of a Startup is evolving. The startup had to search the various moving parts of the business model. In a large business almost everything that had been developed over the years is defined.

A business model comprises four parts, that together form the core of the business. Do the different aspect presents a coherent picture of how the business will operate? Who are the customers? The four important stakeholders of the business model are customer value proposition, technology and operations, profits and go-to-market plan.

- A business model must answer interrelated questions.

- What is the value proposition for the customer?

- How is the customer benefited?

- How will you bring products and services to the market?

- How will you make money from your products and services?

## 4.2 Customer Value Proposition

The customer value proposition describes the unique values that the company has to offer. It answers, what unmet needs the business serves. How do founders know if customers have unmet needs? This is the basic business assumption where most of the new businesses struggle. The Startup should get the initial fundamentals correct to get the basic understanding of the question posed; in the long run, it helps refine the business!

The customer segment to target is another aspect of the customer value proposition. For example, children between the age group of 5 – 12 could be one segment. Their likes, dislikes, habits and purchasing capacity can be explored to promote, offer or refine the product or service. It is important to know whether the segment to serve is new, existing, or re-segmented. The new segment describes that there are no other companies that have launched the product in that segment, but that rarely happens. The existing segment refers to a stratum of people, who are being catered to by existing companies and re-segmented means while the packaging is different, the content is the same.

The four-customer segments are shown below. The bell-shaped curve is bifurcated through four vertical lines, and a product is shown between the lines. The four words written at the vertical lines are innovators, early adopters, early majority and laggard.

## Customer Value Proposition: Segmentation

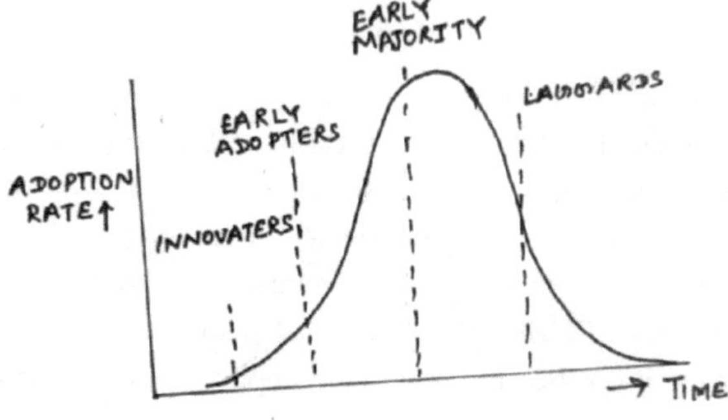


Differentiation is a concept of the customer value proposition which can be in terms of cost or it can be different products in higher order or horizontal differentiation. Higher order or vertical differentiation means higher performance than anyone else can offer in the market, at a higher price. Horizontal means there are some features changes i.e., there are multiple styles to it at the same price. The founder should also ponder on pricing and answer questions like, will it be one time? Per period? Fixed? Variable? Tiered? Bundle based? Skimming or outcome-based? Pricing is discussed more in a later chapter. The founder should be aware of the pricing scheme for the business. He should also consider switching costs and network effects.

## 4.3 Business Plan

*The key tools you will need when you meet the investor.*

The business plan includes all the four factors discussed in the business model including team and hiring, financing, and product. The four elements of the business model do not appear directly in the business plan but may appear indirectly. They should not be revealed to an outsider of the business. Write the business plan as the concept evolves and go through it step by step, do not write it all at once. Refer and improve the plan as more people join, the market evolves or get funding. Updating once a month as the business moves, till the business becomes stable is a good habit.

Every business should have a business plan. It shows how prepared an entrepreneur is. It signals the direction the business is headed. It also helps in mapping the desired vs the current situation. Entrepreneurs can also check the status and analyse the mistakes about where they did wrong? Business plan is a preparation, it's a signal, a map or even an advertising document. It helps us to find the answers in the papers, and teams with business plans are likely to succeed.

No business plan survives the initial contact with the customers. The survival rate of the companies over the years for those who change their business plan is more versus those who don't. Business Plans evolve with time. Many businesses over a span of a few months take a totally different approach than they had initially thought of, but it is good as you have something to learn.

The other reason founders should work on the business plan is that founders' goals should be to get their thoughts into the paper. It helps in creating a hypothesis or assumptions about the business and helps fix the holes in the potential business idea. Adding financials helps to set a goal to meet the demand for cash and improve it on the way. Business plans are just a blueprint that will keep on changing. It's just another story that you move forward with. The elevator pitch, presentation and executive summary are all ways to tell the story.

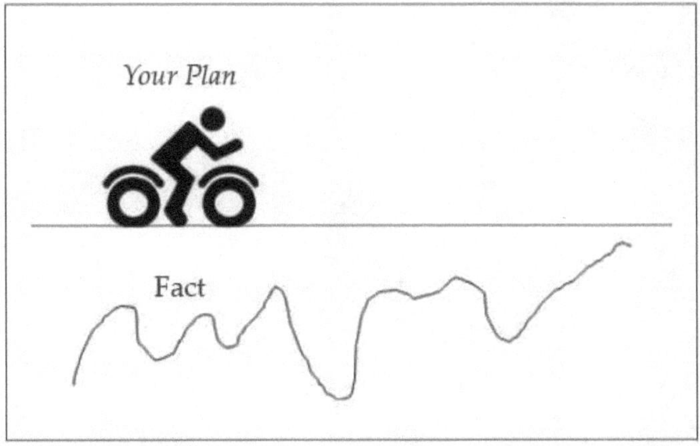


Many consider it as a 20-page document that is prepared to collect dust and has no use. But it gives the much-needed clarity and ticks the boxes of initial basic questions like, how the startup will survive? What is a startup doing differently, that no one else is? It helps the entrepreneur to achieve the milestone and darken the lines which will be compared against actual performance. A successful Startup requires execution and flexibility, further in the course we will see the ultimate validations are the customers that led to profits. In the first stage, entrepreneurs must develop a mini business plan along with an executive summary including sales, marketing and financial projection.

## 4.4 Other business model Development Techniques

*Smart people had already discovered much, you don't need to reinvent the wheel.*

*Customer development model*

Steve Blank focuses to get the initial business model correct through field visits. The product introduction model is not successful according to him, so he built a customer development model. The customer development model has four phases – customer discovery, customer validation, customer creation and company building. The first goal in customer discovery is finding the problem that will solve the customer's pain.

The customer discovery model suggests entrepreneurs go out of the building and start listening to the customer rather than selling. The process gives an insight which helps in refining the process of product development. This is the whole iteration process to discover the customers and validate them. This process is repeated for customer creation and company building.

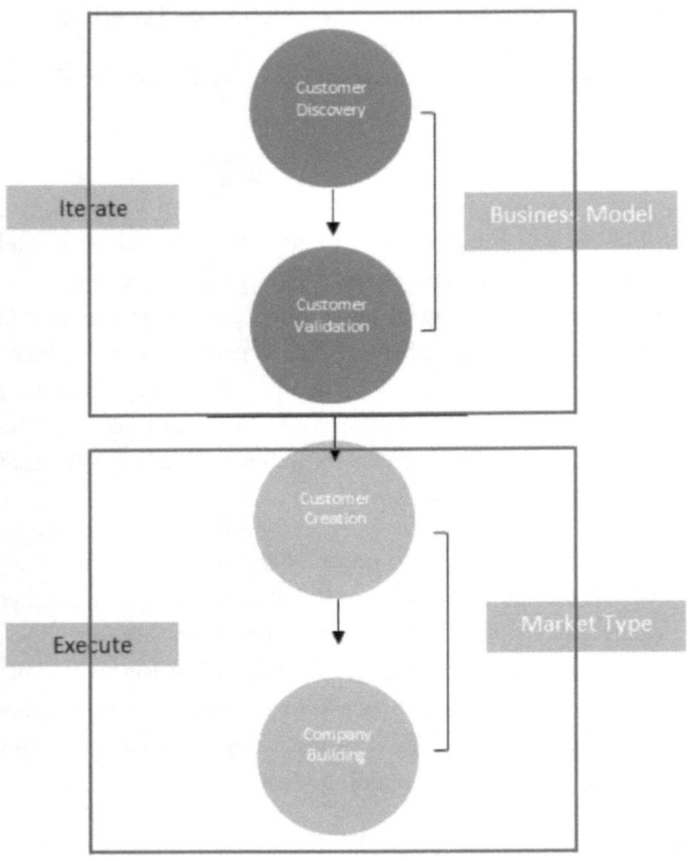


## Lean startups

Eric rise gave the concept of the lean startup. He had a different approach rather than a waterfall approach. He suggested an agile approach. The lean startup makes changes constantly. For example, in websites, programmers make changes in the layout and code thousand times a day to keep moving constantly. So, when you combine the idea of lean startups entrepreneurs are changing everything and rotating things to get the product market fit.

*Hypothesis driven Startup*

Eric Ries coined the term Lean Startup conceptualizing the hypothesis driven approach. The term had an origin in lean manufacturing meaning avoiding waste. The first step in creating a hypothesis driven Startup is to create an objective. Then the initial business model is developed which consists of four elements customer value propositions, go-to-market plan, technology and operation management and cash flow formula or profits. Most businesses are resource constrained when starting up, and deal with uncertainty and risk. A hypothesis driven Startup is a scientific approach to reducing uncertainty. To use this approach entrepreneurs convert their vision using a testing hypothesis and develop a minimum viable product. The process of testing the hypothesis is continued to establish a product market fit. Various assumptions could be related to market, product, and financings which can be converted into valid assumptions. Apart from hypothesis driven Startups, there are other approaches to Startups as well.

A hypothesis driven Startup should be planned carefully, too much iteration and change in a feature of products or services may have devastating consequences. However, once launched, it is like a one-man vehicle and making the changes will be beyond the capabilities and the team will at a greater cost. The concept of launching early and often does also have limitations in specific sectors like drug manufacturing. For instance, drug testing on humans without appropriate testing done prior to that is often prohibited. Also, for the products where the development cycle is long, too much iteration is often not possible. Like, for an electric car manufacturing company changing the models, look, engine and design will often cost millions of dollars. In such cases, a proper thorough analysis can be done by having a 360-degree view before launching and thereafter the products should be considered.

# 5. Hypothesis & Tests

## *5.1 Test in Startups*

### *Assumptions*

Startups are filled with uncertainty. Entrepreneurs assume many things for example the product will be sold at X price. There are two kinds of broad assumptions entrepreneurs make micro and macro. It is advisable that entrepreneur should never focus on wider/macro assumption but should make narrow/micro assumption that is falsifiable and testable. For example, whether the Startup will succeed or not is a wider or macro assumption. This type of assumption will not serve any purpose rather than just increasing the odds. For example, if you assume to fail you will never proceed with the idea. Macro assumptions are just nothing but a sequence of micro works, if we are able to win most of the micro events we will win the macro event. Micro assumptions would be encouraged like a number of customers acquired within six months while the macro like a failure should be discouraged.

The events have to be Mutually Exclusive and Collectively Exhaustive (MECE). Mutually exclusive means two events cannot occur at the same time. In broad terms, mutually exclusive ideas are distinctively separate and not overlapping. For example, in a dice experiment getting a three or a six are mutually exclusive or they cannot happen together. Collective exhaustive means that the set of ideas is inclusive of all possible options. In a dice experiment the events are $\{1, 2, 3, 4, 5, 6,\}$. When making an assumption it is often wise to use the MECE principle to get better results.

Statisticians make assumptions when making models. The most common assumptions are independence, constant variance and approximate normality. The assumption is made to make a model and test the hypothesis. For entrepreneurs, assumptions are crucial to get the model, but in real life circumstances, it's better to validate assumptions before concluding. A startup should also list all the assumptions using the MECE principle. The assumptions should list all the possible (CE) options and the two assumptions should be distinctively separate and not overlapping (ME).

Best businesses make at least 100 contacts to solidify the proof of concept and validate the assumption. Learning and refinement of assumptions through face-to-face interaction are crucial for a person to succeed. This is the only way to test… to get out of the building and meet the customers. The first thing that entrepreneurs should do is check assumptions about customers, partners, segments, and demand. Entrepreneurs should have at least 100 assumptions to prove or disapprove. The major eight topic areas for assumptions are value proposition, positioning, customers, revenue model, business model, go-to-market strategy, marketing, sales and strategy, and partnership strategy. Each topic could have at least twelve to fifteen assumptions.

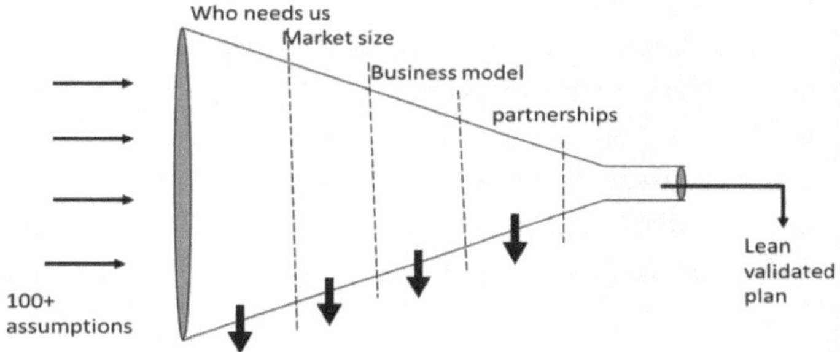


One of the important steps is creating reasonable assumptions. The assumption that young people will buy this, does not meet the criteria of hypothesis formulation! Formulation of assumptions is an art that we will discuss in the next topic. Listing all the assumptions and axing them is one of the first. The business model analysis is iterative an and ongoing process. Often one of the assumptions is dependent upon the other factors. For example, until an entrepreneur figures out the customer segment, customer acquisition cost cannot be figured out. Entrepreneurs should not be detailing too much when making an assumption and creating a hypothesis. Making a quick review of all the parts of the business model and keeping an eye to track metrics is a good way, as entrepreneurs move forwards the processes get streamlined.

Developing a vision is a long-term process which takes shape as time evolves. Entrepreneurs often have little idea when they begin, what the fully developed product will look like. Ideas don't come fully formed, they only become clear as we work on them. The initial objective of hypothesis driven entrepreneurship is to learn about the customers' needs and provide a solution catering to them, instead of launching something directly. The first step is to create a description of the solution or aspiration that the entrepreneur wants to provide to the segment. In other words, these are the unmet needs, and beliefs in future. The entrepreneurs translate their vision of the company into a falsifiable business model hypothesis and then prove or disapprove of the hypothesis to build a Minimal Viable Product.

The process of creating assumptions is continuously repeated until the entrepreneur gets a product market fit. The approach of a hypothesis driven Startup helps mitigate the risk and build a great product. Many businesses fail when they don't create a hypothesis. Startups waste their resources building product that no one cares about. Business model development is a continuous process. Some of the business model hypotheses are interdependent on each other; until the first one is achieved, we can't work on it later; until the market size is estimated, the founder cannot forecast the customers. This is a sort of simplified model which covers the various processes.

## 5.2 Creating Hypothesis

*The assumption that you create to test it!*

Hypothesis[12] is a proposed explanation made on the basis of limited evidence as a starting point for further investigation. The null hypothesis means there is no effect of one variable on another and it's just by chance. The alternatives simply expect that there is a real effect. P value act as a mediator that decides the significance of null and alternative hypothesis on the basis of observed probability. P value is a probability statement which answers the question if the null hypothesis were true what are the chances of observing the same statistics as the experimenter observed in the current experiment? Less P value simply means that the same statistics have a very low probability of getting the same result if we replicate the same experiment and hence, we reject the null. The mnemonic for it is "P is low null must go".

The two important aspects of a hypothesis or making an assumption is testable and falsifiability. Falsifiability means the hypothesis can be rejected in a decisive experiment. Instead of making a statement like 'a customer will like our product' a well proven hypothesis could be drafted as 'our product will gain x number of customers in y number of times at a price range of a to b'. A specific and quantifiable hypothesis is crucial to make it falsifiable.

Statistician do create hypothesis once they have the data. They define the objective. After having the data, we know our objective is to find what we are good at. Hypothesis is a proposed explanation made on the basis of limited evidence as a starting point for further investigation. Null hypothesis means that the observation is just by chance. The alternatives simply tell us that there is a real effect. Sometimes we fail to reject the null that this is by chance. Our null is that all the common patterns that we have gathered are useless. The null is always the boring one. There is no difference: Observed vs expected.

Another example of it is considering the customer acquisition in the customer conversational funnel. For example, X number of customers will be added through the new marketing programme is a better alternative than the number of customers will increase through the marketing campaign. Customer lifetime value and customer acquisition cost are other two metrics that can be used to craft and quantify a hypothesis. Similarly, cohort analysis and A/B testing are the other metrics that can be used to solidify the hypothesis.

To understand it better, let's assume in an educational-based Startup, we consider that the MOOC will allow us to deliver the content outside the platform in a centralised format. So, we could say usually the area that is best to test these sorts of things is either on the technology or operation side or customer value proposition side. It is hard to test. We can use some matric that will help to test, let's think about how we can make this testable. We can write it as – more than 30% of the corporations would choose this over their standard solution. We can say that 30% is falsifiable. Now to make it testable we can say that 30% of the sample HR Professionals shown a wireframe would show purchase intent (prepayment would be better) at the market price x over the market leader's current solution so this is the process that creating the hypothesis should look like! It's hard to get everything tested so we focus on key assumptions only.

## [12] **<u>Hypothesis Testing</u>**

The null hypothesis is denoted by H0 while the alternative is denoted by Ha . The null is typically the condition in which "nothing is going on" (but it doesn't have to be!). Hypotheses can be one or two sided (or "tailed"). $H_0 : \mu = \mu_0$ and $\neq \mu_0$.

- Start with some claims phrased in terms of hypotheses ($H_0$ and $H_a$)

- Collect evidence (Data).

- In statistics, we always assume the null hypothesis is true (Like assuming the defendant is innocent until proven guilty)

- Then we make a decision based on the evidence. If there is sufficient evidence, we reject the null hypothesis (That is, we conclude the defendant is guilty). If there is not enough evidence, then we fail to reject the null hypothesis (that is, we conclude the defendant is not guilty).

1. Mostly tests are standard error counters. They count how many standard errors the null hypothesis mean is away from the sample mean. If the null hypothesis mean is many standard errors (typically greater than 2) away from the sample mean, then the observed data is not in accordance with the null hypothesis, and we believe the data and reject the null.

2. This is the surprise paradigm at work

- Belief: the null hypothesis, $\mu = \mu_0$

- Event of interest: How far $x$ is away from $\mu_0$

- Observed event: $x$ is a long way from $\mu 0$ ; more than $2\sigma/n$ , so it is rare

- Learning: reject $H_0$

### 5.3 False positive and Negative

A hypothesis also comes with errors i.e., false positive and false negative. A false positive means that the hypothesis is confirmed while in reality, it does not hold. Let's say that 100 people get the test for a disease. The test accuracy is 98%. False positive implies that 2% of people who have tested positive may not even have the disease. A false positive testify when it's not, the reasons could be many:

- May be the customer segment chosen is not representative of the mass population.

- Getting a skewed sample size survey of early adopters or enthusiasts can exaggerate the demand while the scenario will be otherwise.

- Testing the products with your near and dear ones also gives false positive results.

False negative means that the hypothesis is disconfirmed while its holds. In the landing page example, the slow landing pages may irritate some of the customers while the overall site is appealing – which can be the case of a false negative. Or it can be a flawed user interface, in which case a usability test can be super helpful. Testing in a series of tests may also help the entrepreneurs to overcome false positives and negatives.

## 5.4 Customer Interview and survey

One of the ways to do an interview and validate the assumption is through a LinkedIn search. Find the relevant people on LinkedIn, write and ask about the assumptions or the product or services that you have to offer. The other way is through Google AdWords (Use digital marketing survey), you can pay and get real feedback on how many people are interested in the product and who is your target segment.

| What Customer Interview is Good for | What Customer Interview is Bad at |
|---|---|
| • Customer interview is great for finding out what people like or don't like about the product. So, you can ask what worked for the customers. Does this solution work for you?<br>• On the other hand, the customer interviews are good for finding out about the current solution, finding out why the current solution has been chosen, and for getting a sense of customer environment. | • Customer interview is really bad for predicting future actions. Whether you will switch or not is a really hard question to ask! Some people ask questions, assuming the market does not change, assuming there is no competitor. Too many assumptions cannot make sense at all.<br>• Customer interviews are also bad for forecasting demand. If some people are enthusiastic, they may buy something, but other people may not.<br>• Customer interviews are also bad for figuring out pricing and figuring out product features. You will have the worst product features when you try customer interviews to fix them. |

## 5.5 Personal Visit

A personal visit is to gauge the existing market and customers. It offers benefits over other qualitative or quantitative tools including the opportunity to discuss in detail the various nuances with the supreme end user. The first task in a personal visit is to target the segment and identify the early adopters of the product for the visit. Classifying at least 50 sets of customers who are willing to give interviews would be enough. A convenience sample could also be taken, and friends and family will be given the opportunity to interview. However, the entrepreneurs should be wary that, the sample taken is representative of the whole population. A sampling frame could be better to decide which are the segments for a personal visit. The following things can be considered:

- When planning a visit make sure you don't impose too many agendas on the same visit. A well-planned visit should have at the most two or three research objectives.

- Probing is one of the major tools to extract information from the customers without getting biased opinions.

- A moderator should be kept and the interviews could be recorded.

- The interview time has to be around one hour as after one hour it would be hard to retain focus and the interviewee may lose interest.

- Repo building should be done initially.

- Yes/no questions should be avoided. The interview should be exploratory with the use of how, why and what, as these are better means to probe the interviewee.

- Entrepreneurs should choose a place to interview with minimum distractions; make better seating arrangements for comfort during the interview.

## 5.6 Online Methods

Various other online methods could be used given that the customer has an online presence.

- Facebook and AdWords can be used with clearly defined problem descriptions.

- Twitter can be used to tweet customers who have used similar products directly.

- Emails, google alerts, and craigslist can also be used to track and get online feedback from customers.

- Personal referral, alumni network, and previous company employees could also be a good way to get customers.

- Seminars, trade shows, conferences and other networking events could also be alternatives for reaching customers.

- LinkedIn can also be used for B2B customers.

- Cold calling through phone calls could also be done to fix an appointment for a personal interview or describe the product or service.

*Survey*

One of the most important aspects of the survey is a sample. If samples are not representative, then the survey is useless. In a survey, we make sure to ask good questions.

A survey can be misleading but doing it the right way can be hard.

## 5.7 Test in Startups

*Early Diagnosis of failure*

When statisticians build a model, they run some diagnoses before proceeding. For example, statisticians check the normality assumptions; check residuals; plot the data through a scatter plot to check if everything is making sense. Histograms and correlation matrices are other tools that help. No statistician can produce a conclusive result without checking all the facts and assumptions. It's a complete stepwise continuous trial method because we can't fit a model if the assumptions are wrong. Similarly, the entrepreneurs should use some tools to check the model and assumption, there are various tools that can provide insight. Tools like survey, A/B testing, and hypothesis building helps in rectifying the problems and validating the assumption. We will discuss in the coming few topics all the tools that help the diagnosis of the Startup assumptions.

### *5.8 Smoke test*

*Let the smoke pass through the actual prototype!*

The smoke test is good for testing MVP. It has its origin in ancient Rome. The process involves forcing smoke through new plumbing to detect the leak. Smoke tests are good for products that are not yet developed operationally and functionally. It deals with the idea of a product; you set an option for people without showing the product. The modern system considers it as the first test to see if the assembled product is working properly.

The entrepreneurs using the smoke test give an online description of the product they want to make, to the customers, and ask if they want to buy or use the same product or not. For example, you may have seen a sign up for a product. these are kind of classic smoke tests. It's called a landing page and then you will have to sign up. When launching a web-based business, to test and gauge the features of the online services, landing pages are often prepared to test among the initial customers.

Various methods can be used without developing the product like a newsfeed, signup, purchase intent, etc. if reasonable people show interest, then entrepreneurs have some confidence to build on the product. It gives an overview of what the customer base looks like, but for sure it does not validate the demand. If none of the customers or limited customers show interest then may be the entrepreneurs need to consider the problem description or maybe they are moving in the wrong direction.

A short description in the form of a video explaining the features of the products is also a better alternative since the product is in a nascent phase and its use is not properly defined. The entrepreneur can also ask for purchase commitment through a letter of intent after showing the product description. It is called a dry test, Kickstarter has ample funding for a project where the entrepreneur has listed the project details which is in a nascent stage, to ask for funding, if enough funding and credibility of the entrepreneur is maintained, then the projects take off.

## 5.9 Usability testing

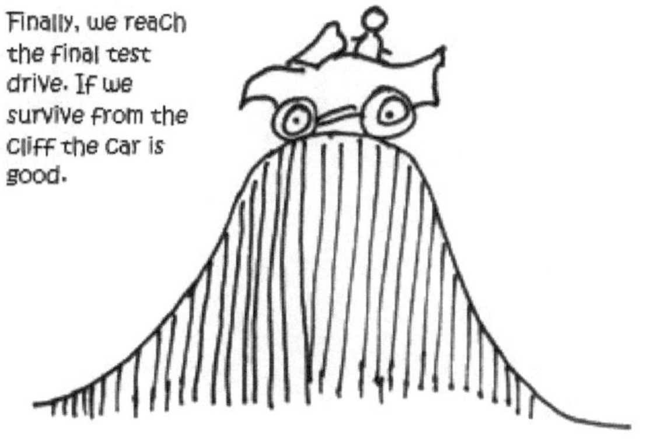


We often learn about the product better and more quickly by using it. This method lets the customer interact with the product. It is proven that 80% of the major problems in new products can be identified by a sample of fewer than five customers. It rules out the risk of a bad product being made. Usability test matters and it's a useful test to do. The usability test asks the customers to complete the specific task using the prototype developed. The goal is to identify the loopholes in the prototype.

The usability test can be done at any stage of product development. It is also useful in collecting data to check the actual response of the prototype when interacting with the user. The goal of the test is to fix the holes and reiterate them to make a usable product. The benefits of the test are that within a small sample size, all the errors in the prototype can be found. The experiment could be recorded at the same time.

## 5.10 Split test or A/B test

*Which is better A or B?*

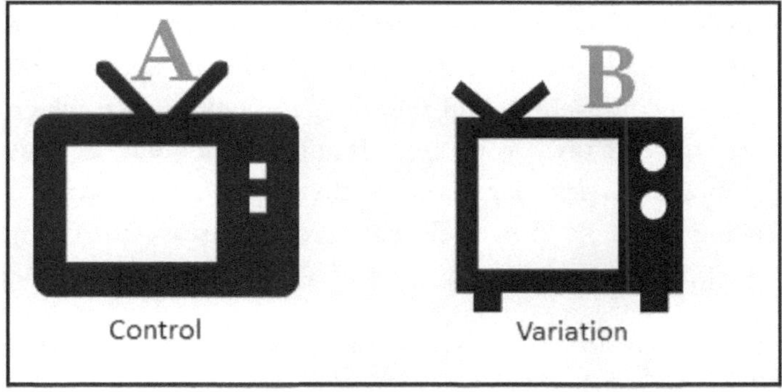



Split test deals with testing different versions of the same product to the consumer at a time. Web-based split test is easy and convenient to use. Let's say when designing a website, you have two designs of web pages and you want to test which design is better. You show virtually both the webpages to the user, asking which design of the webpage you like and gathering the response of the customers. When conducting a split test some statistical knowledge is useful to draw the inference. A/B testing is also known as the two sample T test. All T tests are standard error counters. They measure how far the mean is from the centre. If the observed mean is greater than two, then reject the null, citing the result as rare, not repeatable.

The idea is, I don't know what the answer is! I will test multiple options at once to see what works better. The best example is during the Obama campaign there were five possible opening messages that people were shown. You came to the website and were shown an auto-playing movie, Obama speeches, pictures of rallies, pictures of his family, pictures of the flag and all these sorts of things to argue about choosing from. Another example is four options on the webpage are shown all with the same purpose, join us now, learn more, and sign up. So, you came to the website and the picture is randomized which are the pictures you saw. It turns out that in this combination learning more is the highest percentage of liking. It is so powerful that it can increase profit by multiple folds.

Statistician do create hypothesis once they have the data. They define the objective. After having the data, we know our objective is to find what we are good at. Hypothesis is a proposed explanation made on the basis of limited evidence as a starting point for further investigation. Null hypothesis means that the observation is just by chance. The alternatives simply tell us that there is a real effect. Sometimes we fail to reject the null that this is by chance. Our null is that all the common patterns that we have gathered are useless. The null is always the boring one. There is no difference: Observed vs expected.

# 6. Managing Teams

## *6.1 Hierarchical Setup*

*Hiring and retaining the right team is crucial. Have you ever wondered what kind of people are most worthy of a Startup?*

*Hierarchy of the speed*

## *Interviewing*

## *Hiring: The Interview*

**Interview panel:**As many people as possible (3 - 5 is fine)

Definitely ask historical questions:

- Walk through each job

- Tell me about a time when

Potentially ask behavioural/hypothetical questions:

- 

  What would your former subordinates say about you?

- What company do you admire? How would you compete against it?

Think hard before hiring someone from McKinsey or Microsoft.

**Avoid illegal questions:**Race, religion, gender, national origin, age, military service eligibility, veteran status, sexual orientation, family or disability

Make the interviewing experience as great and fair as possible

Like hiring and retaining an employee is difficult without raising the funds. Most of the founders work individually initially.

## 6.2 Balancing Teams: Juggling the role, reward and relationship

The three important pillars for building a team are role, reward and relationship. There is always a struggle in a new team for roles and rewards. While the third one, relationship, when hampered, will sink the boat of a Startup.

- It is always better to have an explicit conversation with the team rather than face a crisis later. Decisions like equity, roles and responsibilities should be disposed off, early.

- The relationship is the single most important factor that can blow up the role and reward. If the founding team blows up early, it will not take much time to wrap up.

- The role is the other important aspect, as the business grows, clarity of roles in the decision-making process is of utmost importance. Slowly but carefully there had to be a mechanism and common understanding, if it is formalized on paper or in agreement, even better.

- Everybody has their own interest in starting a business, hence the rewards or perks and the ultimate factor and can make or break relationships.

*Balancing a founding Teams*

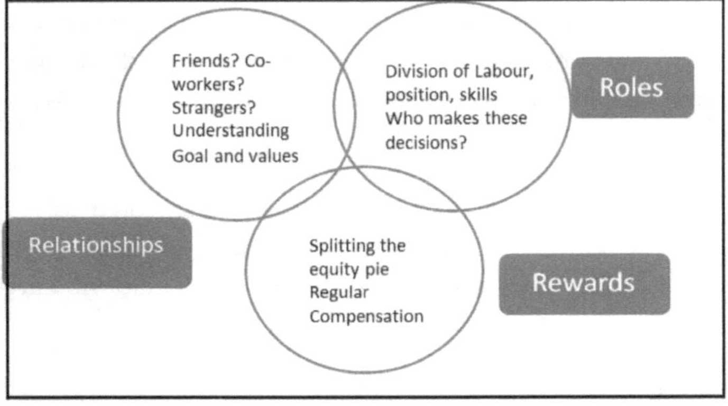

## 6.3 Attracting talent

Most of the time it is difficult to attract talent because nobody wants to be associated with something that has no visibility. The stake or perks that are given to the team often matters a lot which is really difficult to maintain during the early times.

Hiring Sources

- Hiring decisions initially take place by using your network i.e., by shaking your tree.

- Events and contests are better ways of getting the right people on the team which can be considered in the later phases.

- Startups need the best people to work early on; often one of the easiest ways to attract talent is by providing internships to premium school graduates.

| | | Specificity of Skills | |
|---|---|---|---|
| | | High | Low |
| Prominence of Role | High | Headhunters go after competitors | Advertise with good filters |
| | Low | You go after key people at competitors | Advertising, University Visits, etc. |

## *How to hire?*

- Hire A people: As highlighted in the book The Art of the Start 2.0 by Guy Kawasaki 'A people attract A people'. One of the reasons that happen is because 'A' people have 'A' networks so that will get you more 'A' people. The second thing is natural attractiveness.

- Founders should understand the hiring decisions and understand the role properly for each hiring decision it makes.

- Hiring decisions should be made based on what specific skills are needed and how prominent their role is.

- When looking for skills entrepreneurs should be looking for someone who can build synthetic DNA compounds i.e., we are looking for specificity.

- For high end people you need headhunters and for low end, you call them directly.

- There are two classes of employees one is, the middle managers and the other is, the innovators.

- Some of the initial employees are more worthy than others.

## *6.4. The art & science of human capital valuation*

Hiring is often important for team building; it also becomes crucial as most entrepreneurs have not been involved in hiring in the past. The best way to introduce the hiring process is through interesting research done by See smart, 1998, The art and science of human capital valuation that helps explore the hiring technique in a startup environment. What the study found was that there were five basic study techniques people use in order to interview people in these environments – airline pilot, the infiltrator, the artist, the sponge and the prosecutor.

The first one is an artist, artists are the people who do not believe in data, they believe that they are able to judge people based on years of experience and knowledge. The Internal Rate of Return (IRR) for this approach is 25%. This is low IRR and not much effective and should be avoided. This technique simply relies based on their personal judgement to evaluate a candidate.

The sponge has a different approach, they deal with many kinds of data, take work samples, do interviews, and might ask hypothetical questions. The hope is that they get some information out of these long processes that could be useful. Again, the IRR for this approach is even less than for artists i.e., 20%. Just gathering data without any purpose doesn't help its terms of determining very much, whether the candidate is good or bad.

The third approach is the prosecutor. A prosecutor aggressively asks questions to candidates hoping to make them break under pressure like a lawyer. Basically, they try to get the candidate under stress and break down in order to get the true answer. Surprisingly this approach is the worst and has an IRR of just 10% on average.

The fourth one is the spy or infiltrator approach, in this approach basically, they live in with the candidate, travel with the candidate, share hotels with them, they have a meeting with the client along with the candidates. Unsurprisingly this approach is terrific and is the most valued with an IRR of around 100%. It's very effective in picking the right candidate with an entrepreneurial mindset. It requires a huge amount of time and is a difficult job to do.

The next is airline pilots. They depend upon the checklist, they stick to what they plan, checking things moving forward… like are we looking for someone who has previous sales experience? Are we looking for someone who has previous programming experience? They look for characteristics that are needed in the job and check them off. The IRR for this approach is 80%.

The spy approach is not practical, which makes the airline pilot the second-best approach. So, now you know airline pilot is the best approach, but how to do it? The interviewee can come up with a score card. In the score card approach, you go through everything you need for the job and you write down your features, be specific when writing down the characteristics. They also need to coordinate with other interviewees, all sharing the same scorecard and asking different questions. Then you think of screening that will help you gather information, you can meet people over a phone call, or lunch. You can also assign prework, prework reveals information about how they actually work.

Don't interview alone you need multiple points of view, if you don't have three to five people in your company, then you can pull your friends and family who help you out. A good predictor of the future is past performance. So, ask historical questions like, 'walk me through each of your jobs', and ask them to speak of a time in their job when they did something that is of interest,  ask them to talk of a time when they showed leadership under pressure. Don't hear the story, make an interactive conversation. Ask what they did, why they did it, why people react, what the boss did… Potentially you can ask a hypothetical question like what company they admire.

## 6.5 Allocating Title and Advisory Board

*The tag that impresses people more than their job.*

Entrepreneurs generally make mistakes initially by putting their name as a CEO without reaching any milestone. Instead, the focus should be on the target to achieve, assess the capabilities the teams have, what core skills Startups need further to strengthen and what mechanism they use to develop them. Can they hire someone or if they can be outsourced? The financing team should also be given due diligence, someone who understands the intricacies of the finance and who has raised the funding before it could be an asset to the organization. Below are a few pointers on having a board.

- Entrepreneurs should also be considered due diligence when allocating titles to their fellow team members. Making an early decision without the proper assessment could be fatal. Relationship damages are more devastating initially at the same time it also reflects on the team performance.

- Often forming a board and advisors within the launch of a few months of a Startup is not a great idea.

- Also, if managed to attract a good board and advisors it is the sole responsibility of the founder to fix priorities, schedule meetings, pitch agendas and send regular updates and timelines that are planned to move ahead. In most cases, founders fail to gain the advantage either through disconnect or by not making necessary follow-ups.

- It is often difficult to attract a board or director who can add tremendous value to the team. A board hired early, often outweigh the benefits and flexibility of a short team to move ahead the curve and develop products and services, it could be better if an entrepreneur could gain some ground before formalising the team and advisors.

- If a venture moves to raise the capital it often requires a substantial amount of effort to dictate the term sheet. Removing anyone from the board is often the hardest part, especially in the early phases which burn the bridges.

- Paying compensation and the fiduciary role often outplay the crucial role that the initial founding team can play. While there is also a major difference between the board of directors and advisor.

- Advisors are not legally bound in the company while the directors are. Also, directors have a fiduciary role while advisors fill the gap in the team by providing the necessary skills needed for the Startup.

- During the early phases, the Board of Advisors (BOA) is a better alternative than the Board of Directors (BOD), also equity needs to be distributed, which varies between 0.1 to 0.5%.

- A good BOA adds value to the firm at later stages when raising the funding BOD can be put together.

- BOA does not have any formal power and can add much-needed value. Also, a specialised advisory board helps like customer advisory which will take major decisions in the customer development process, sales funnel, market research, refining the assumption, target segmentation and pricing to name among a few.

## 6.6 Cliff Vesting

Attracting good cofounders and team is necessary. One of the ways to distribute equity to a team is through cliff vesting.

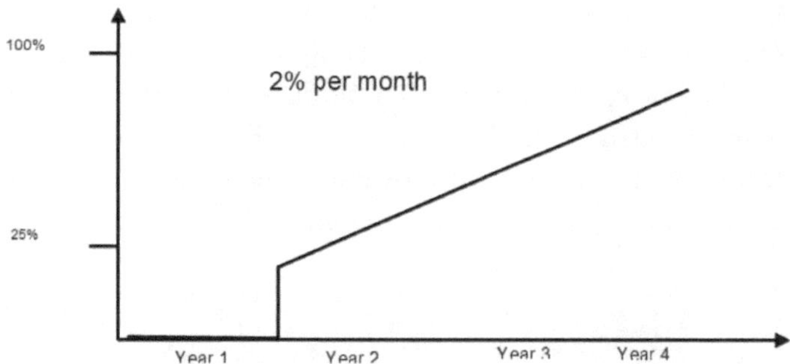


team is through cliff vesting.

In cliff vesting people get equity in the startup on completion of a certain time in the Startup. A typical vesting may span four years with one year as the cliff. A one-year cliff means that the person will not get any shares vested until one year. After completion of a year, the person will receive 25% of the total shares vested which occurs every month. Cliff vesting assures the employees have stock, but the team must work hard to get it. Typically, the shares vested are at the rate of 2% per month after a year, till it gets all the shares allocated to him within a span of forty-eight months.

One of the biggest benefits of cliff vesting is that, if people don't work out within a year Startups are not out with too many small shareholders. To further protect the shareholding in founding teams, a certain clause could be added to the cofounder agreement. If a co-founder leaves the company in the initial stages, she will only get a small portion of the shares. Shares will be given only after a specified period of working for the company. If a co-founder leaves the company at an initial stage, it is difficult for the startup to survive and it burdens other co-founders. A mechanism of vesting schedule can be built so that the cofounder has to stay with the company to get back all the shares owned by him in the company.

| S.No | Title | Range (%) |
|---|---|---|
| 1 | CEO | 5-10 |
| 2 | COO | 2-5 |
| 3 | VP | 1-2 |
| 4 | Board Member | 1 |
| 5 | Director | 0.4-1.25 |
| 6 | Lead Engineer | 0.25-1 |
| 7 | Engineer | 0.33-0.66 |
| 8 | Junior Engineer | 0.2-0.33 |

The people associated with the company could be given equity based on their roles. The above table depicts the various level of an equity offering to the CEO, COO, VP and employees. The distribution of shares could range depending on the designation and importance of the role the person plays in the organization.

## 6.7 Negotiations

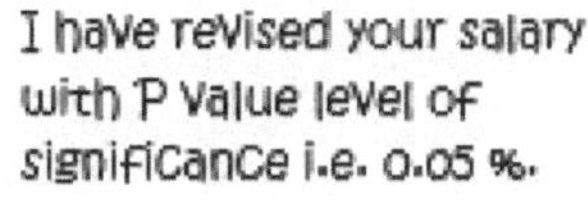

Entrepreneurs have to do a lot of negotiations with employees, partners, VCs, and cofounders and hence it becomes an important skill. Negotiation skills can bring a difference. Negotiation is like a double-edged sword which can easily create friction between the two parties however if done properly it can enlarge the profit pie rather than split it.

It is always considered a zero-sum game; however, entrepreneurs should focus on win-win situations. A one-time transaction in which someone buys an asset for a price is considered a zero-sum game. The negotiations are also relative as one founder may be interested in getting a bigger pie of equity but another may be in control, someone may want a greater compensation while the other may look for long-term prospects with the company. Experienced negotiators look for values.

Founders have to deal with problems of HR issues and manage employees; being first-time founders they don't know how to deal with it, which can lead to conflict and subsequently exit of employees. These are some of the rules which are suggested when dealing with it.

- Separate yourself from your business. Your business failure is not your personal failure most businesses fail when they start. Emotions prevent you from really seeing what is happening.

- Separate the problem with the people: Always try to clarify perceptions and separate emotions from the actual problem! Knowing the interest of the other person can help immensely in negotiations. An entrepreneur should look for interest rather than title and positions. The entrepreneur should know each other properly about their interest and gains which is crucial to take a meaningful negotiation, otherwise, it is worthless.

- It is also meaningful to talk about what the other party is bringing to the table and evaluate its worthiness for the start-up whether it is hiring an employee or choosing a logistic partner.

- An entrepreneur should also decide early upon the title, compensation, equity, control and decision-making capability in form of a written agreement before moving forward.

- For any negotiation to succeed trust is the ultimate deciding factor which can make or break the negotiation, be sure to gain the trust early on as in later stages it would be difficult. Gaining the trust early will help entrepreneurs move on to other things like equity, compensation and further things to consider.

# 7. Marketing

*The art of selling ideas, developing a prototype and fundamentals of marketing.*

## 7.1 The fundamental of marketing

Social media networks and various other micro-engaging platforms had opened a wide array of possibilities to connect with the consumer. Digital marketing techniques especially post Covid have drastic changes. However, the fundamentals of marketing remain at the centre to keep, grow and retain customers. Often without understanding, the various nuance of marketing marketers found it difficult to allude to customers.

The fundamentals of marketing start with the 5 Cs of marketing, which narrow down to STP and 4 Ps. They are the core and are considered the backbone of marketing!! Covering everything in marketing will be beyond the scope of the book.

### 5C's

The five pillars help understand the environment in which a business operates! 5 Cs of marketing are customers, competitors, collaborators, company and context! The customers, competitors and company are self-explanatory.

Collaborators are the people or partners of your company it could be your distributors, suppliers or media partners. Collaborators create a coherent picture for the company as an important pillar. Context is the environment in which the business operates, it could be political, economic, or cultural. The context varies the way business operates.

## STP

STP stand for Segmentation, Targeting and Positioning!! The segment is the strata of your customers. For example, let's say for a bar of soap, one customer like green soap bars and another may like a red bar. Consumers may have different willingness to pay and the income, geography and social status they belong to can vary. The whole market could be segmented into different strata. One segment may want to invest twenty rupees and the other may want to invest ten rupees. The company can choose the segment to cater to. Businesses may choose to target a certain segment of customers, based on how lucrative the target There may be a number of companies that may offer a product to the same segment, and hence positioning comes into the picture, it's just a tweak that the company does to position its brand and differentiate it from its competitors!!

## 4P's

The last piece of marketing is the four P's which are widely known as product, price, place and promotion. Product is your offering; the place is the location of the product and promotion is the means through which we create awareness or advertisement to improve the visibility and sales of a product.

## 7.2 Pricing

Businesses, when launched seldom have an idea how much to charge for the product. Setting a price is an iterative process. Businesses, that set higher pricing don't attract customers and lower prices can erode profit margin. The pricing insight window is available for business owners before the launch of the product. Pricing should be set correctly during the Startup launch. After entrepreneurs launch the product the window to set price gets closed and the customer develops a fixed mindset for the price of your product. If entrepreneurs try to increase the price after the launch, they receive a setback from the customers.

Pricing can be set in various ways for example customer-focused pricing, supplier focussed pricing, or competitor focussed pricing. However, customer focussed pricing which is based on optimal pricing is the best method to choose, for new products. Supplier focussed pricing deals with cost plus pricing while competitor focussed pricing focuses on setting your price based on your competitors rather than value creation. Also, competitor focussed pricing does not include the newness and innovation in the product offering.

Customer focussed pricing can take two ways, either we can ask the customer for their willingness to pay and can run a statistical test. Secondly, pricing can be gauged if we deeply understand the customer's decision-making process. When we ask customers we can use Van Westendorp, pairwise comparison or conjoint analysis to do the statistical test. In the case of decision-making, the voice of the customer and observation method could be used to gauge the price.

| | |
|---|---|
| *Need Recognition* | The first step is to recognise the need. |
| *Search for Information* | Search the information or products to satisfy the need. |
| *Evaluation of Alternative* | The consumer evaluates all the products that satisfy the need. |
| *Purchase Decision* | Make the appropriate purchase decision. |
| *Post Purchase Evaluation* | Consumer analyses if he has made the right decision, he may face cognitive dissonance if he thinks he made the wrong decision. |

For customer decision making it is crucial to measure customer knowledge and interest. B2B business should focus on the customer decision making process to set the price. B2B index can be a good way to measure the focus of the businesses. The higher the index the higher B2B focussed the business is! The decision making process can be understood in major five steps – need recognition, search for information, evaluation of alternatives, purchase decision, post-purchase evaluation.

The other way to do the pricing is by pricing ladder. A pricing ladder is a product strategy that involves supplying several product versions at different quality and price points. In monadic everybody gets the question once and gets random pricing. But you must get your questions right otherwise it is useless.

Bundled pricing and two-tier pricing is a famous part among investors. In bundled pricing, we sell a bouquet or group of products and sell them at a single price and two-tier pricing companies want to extract more of the consumer surplus, by using a pricing scheme made up of two parts for example the machine and the liquid refill to kill the mosquitos.

*Conjoint Analysis*

Conjoint analysis is used in the case of new product development. It combines different attributes of the products and estimates the value that the customer attaches to the attribute. For example, a restaurant chain can have various attributes such as ambience, food, staff behaviour, billing system, music and others. The researcher can make two or more combinations of attributes and ask the customer which of these they prefer.

Conjoint Choice task

*Apple Vs Dell: Which of these smartphones would you buy?*

| | *Brand* | **Apple** | **Dell** | |
|---|---|---|---|---|
| Attributes | *Screen Size* | 5inch | 6 inches | *Level of Attribute* |
| | *Colour* | Black | White | |
| | *Price* | $1200 | $1100 | |
| | *Product Concepts to choose from* | | | |

Conjoint analysis prepares various bundles of attributes and asks the consumer to rate on a Likert scale through a survey. As individual attributes can be misleading as enthusiasts or laggards are going to rate it as per the bias they have. On the basis of quantitative analysis, the preference of each respondent is analysed by examining the pattern. Conjoint analysis helps define the various value proposition and it also helps determine which attributes are most and least valued among the customers.

*Monadic pricing*

The cheap way of exploring pricing is monadic pricing. In monadic pricing surveyor ask each respondent about the willingness to pay at a different price point. For example, how willing would you be to subscribe to a service for $20 per month that sends you a sweater every month like one of those shown below (Shows the picture) and we record the number which is a different number for each one.

## 7.3 Customer Lifetime Value

Customer lifetime value is the process of understanding how customers yield revenue over some time horizon. It is the total worth to a business of a customer over the whole period of their relationship of purchasing. If a customer bought a $40 present on Christmas from the same company for the last 10 years, the CLV has been $400. This looks simple however in bigger companies it gets complex.

It could be calculated through the discounted present value of variable contribution, revenue minus variable cost earned over the life of a customer relationship with the company. Or simply it can be given by

**CLV = customer value X average customer lifespan**

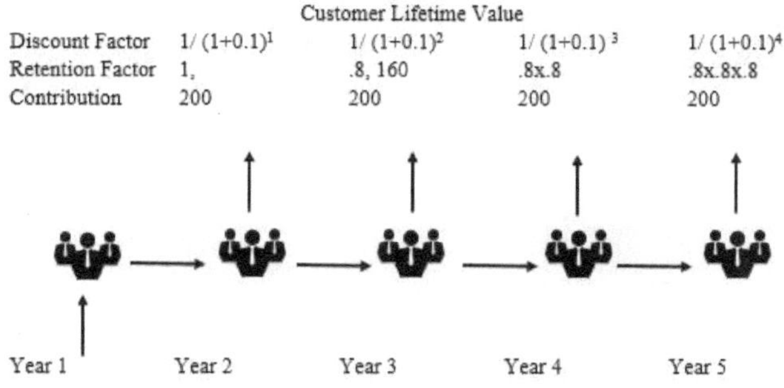



The cash flow per customer minus the discounted present value and the customer retention factor gives the lifetime value of the customer. The contribution of a customer could be calculated as revenue earned from all the

customers minus the variable cost in a given year. The average life of a customer could also be calculated by the formula 1/x where "x" is the annual customer churn rate. To calculate the customer acquisition cost, we can calculate the total sales minus the retention cost.

CLV is closely associated with another metric – CAC (customer acquisition cost). CAC is the money a company invests in acquiring a new customer, for example, the cost of advertising, discounts, coupons, etc. Customer lifetime value cannot be interpreted fully without taking into account the CAC. For example, if the CLV is $1,000 and it costs $1,000 to acquire then there is no revenue or additional benefit to the company.

## 7.4 Advice on selling and marketing

### 1. Gladiators

There are two types of sales people needed in the business. The first kind is gladiators, also known as solo hunters, who go away, don't check in frequently, and bring back customers having sold the product. This approach is needed during the start of a business. The second kind is professional sales people. They are usually trained at a big company; they require support staff to succeed and drive sales. They are good at taking orders and building relationships at the same time but are also expensive to hire. Businesses need different people at different stages of Startup initially gladiator and later professional sales.

### 2. You need both art and science to sell

The true marketer will always look not only at quants but also at poets. If we just look at the number, we will miss the insight which is as valuable as numbers. The problem with quantities is that they don't reveal the intensity of love or hatred. For example, I have one friend who just drove 160 km to attend my wedding when I was getting married. Thus you may have just one customer who is passionate about what you make. While there are hundreds of viewers, there are no buyers.

The intensity of love or passion for products can't be measured while the number of customers who bought the product can. Companies that had been able to create a strong brand, make sure they have passionate followers. Entrepreneurs should design metrics to measure the intensity too. Surveys, focus group discussions, and ethnographic studies are the ultimate tools that can give better insight into the passion for a product by the consumer.

*3. How can you validate demand?*

A letter of Intent (LOI) is a useful tool to validate demand. The entrepreneurs can show the prototype of the product to the customers and ask if they want to purchase the product or not. A signed letter of intent in which the potential customer agrees to buy the product can also be used to raise the working capital. Although it's not legally binding, LOI signifies a strong signal towards the potential customer's validation and demand for a product.

## 7.5 Pitching your idea

*Pitch it hard, get it done.*

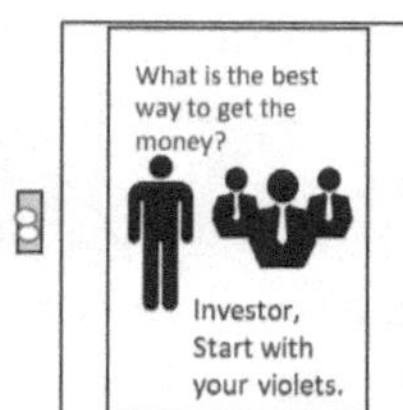

- Prototype pitches are alternatives to elevator pitches. Prototype pitches focus more on what your offering to the world is. It's a demonstration of the product or service and provides minute details that entrepreneurs bring.

- ***Passion versus preparedness:***Don't just tell stories, but also show your audience the stuff (product/offering) at the same time… even if it is half complete. Prototypes initiate action which creates credibility to your words and what you pitch; it can make a big difference. The content is what matters more than the passion. There has been some research work on passion versus preparedness. The study measures the observer's energetic style, rich body language, facial expression, gesture and tone. The outcome is that the preparedness for the venture weighs more than just words and gestures. The audience is sceptical; show them the stuff which adds value to your words. For example, not only the prototype that the entrepreneurs show to the public, but the institution he studied in, or his clothes (like a doctor's couch) and experience in the field of the Startup launched, further strengthens the credibility of the entrepreneur.

- During pitches hook the audience quickly; demonstrate what you can do. Don't just pitch the prototype and leave them wanting more information.

- The content and the credibility matter most in the pitches. Stories attract people, don't forget to explore the space you are entering with a short story with pain points which act as a hook for the investor.

- Pitches are literally the most common tool that entrepreneurs use to entreat people. It is such an important tool that you must get it right to attract or sell your idea. The pitches could be crafted for any Startup entering the space. These are some of the pitches that carry strong brand recognition.

- Follow the KISS principle, Keep it Simple and Stupid. Your idea should be simple so that it could be explained to a 16-year-old. It's important for your audience to understand the concept. If I am pitching to a VC and using technical terms that they don't understand they will not listen to it. They are not going to ask about the technicalities of the venture. So, it's often better to start with simple rather than technical. It's Okay to have a few technical words. It is easy to end up in a situation where the audience just doesn't understand, so simplify and simplify your pitches.

- A summary of the business should be prepared so that it prompts the right question. If the investor is still asking questions like how you plan to do things, it is a signal that they still need clarity in the business idea and the pitch had failed to communicate the basic understanding. The Elevator pitch's goal is all about getting someone to start the conversation. An entrepreneur should be wary that he must make sure that the investor doesn't ask questions that are basic stuff about the concept or idea.

- An entrepreneur should pitch according to the investor he has chosen. For example, when pitching for VCs the money they invest initially, the exit strategy (which is around $50 million in return) and due diligence are of importance. Also, the control of the company when setting a board should be considered. In the same way, when raising funds from the angel or banker the pitch should be customised, as banks do not prefer risky businesses and angels are okay with it. Thorough research is need to be done before pitching according to the investor's preference, portfolio, and size of investment with the risk tolerance.

### *How to write pitches?*

Elevator pitches are necessary, rather than just dwelling on a 100-page business plan, a short and crispy presentation on what you do, is preferred by investors. This is the pitch that is suggested by Guy Kawasaki in his book 'The Art of the Start: The Time-Tested, Battle-Hardened Guide for Anyone Starting Anything.

…………… for target audience……. who……has a need……………. the …product name…………..is a……product category………. that……offers a key benefit……………

unlike…competitor                                                    or substitute……………………..we……are different in a key way…………

*An example of a pitch for Tesla*

*For* **wealthy individuals and car fans***who* **want a high-end sport that is environmentally friendly, the tesla roadster***is an* **electric car***that* **delivers unprecedented performance without damaging the environment.***Unlike* **Ferrari and Proche***we* **offer amazing performance without direct carbon emission.**

## 7.6 Bootstrapping

- Bootstrapping is one of the ways through which Startups groom organically. Many entrepreneurs dream of bootstrapping and getting early cash flow rather than giving up a lot of stakes to the investor.

- Bootstrapping helps the entrepreneur maintain full control and steady growth of the venture.

- Sometimes more money imbibes more mistakes, unnecessary expenses and a team that is not needed at the juncture. However, at the same time, cash-starved businesses never reach the implementation stage. Bootstrapping does not only give cash to the business, but it also stress tests the business idea. While in a booming market, it is quite easy to raise external funding but difficult to sell the product or service.

- The major drawback of bootstrapping is that the businesses that have good growth potential do require ample resources. For example, web-based businesses or eCommerce which is difficult to grow organically or are difficult to bootstrap. External funding may boost the businesses with the necessary infrastructure, manpower, operations and marketing support which are crucial for fast-paced business.

- Bootstrapping is also sometimes supplemented through no salaries to the founder, side hustle, own cash injection, and may operate from a garage. Also, it is sometimes difficult to bootstrap and compete.

- Founders should gauge properly at what stage they should switch bootstrap to other sources of funds. They should realistically asses the time and resources they have to get ahead of the curve.

# 8. Prototyping

*MVP is the first step, everybody's MVP looked ugly when they first made them whether it's Apple's or Google's.*

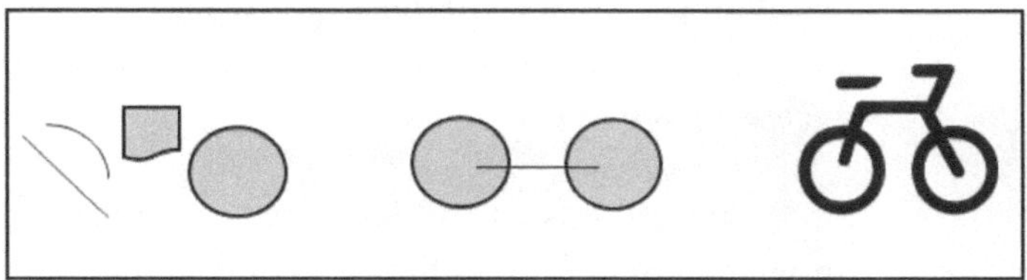

## 8.1 Minimum Viable Product with maximum customer acquisition

*Customer is key to building a great MVP.*

- Statistical modelling gives us the word 'Parsimony' which simply means frugal. Entrapment should build a model that should be as simple as possible but not simpler. When making a product, entrepreneurs should focus on fundamentals rather than building a complex model. The lean principle and MVP all follow the same principle. Complexity increases the odds that the task will never get completed. That's why we build a prototype first just before dumping millions of dollars. Make a paper boat before you make a real boat, see if this works. It will at least give a good understanding of the thing that are closely associated, the problems you face and the challenges. The more complicated your model is the more complicated your decision.

- MVP tests the hypothesis quickly and with the least possible expenditure of resources.

- Developing a minimum viable product as soon as the Startup launches the business, is necessary so that the founder has the time to test and validate the business model.

- MVPs are replicas of products that resemble the product closely but at the same time, they can reduce the cycle time and iteration of product development phases creating something worthy based on customer feedback.

- The best way to learn is to launch early and often. Rather than getting into a continuous feedback and analysis loop, it is often encouraged to get the task done and then reiterate. Investing too much time in something that no one cares about is often useless for the company. Building the smallest set of features and testing it is a better approach rather than building everything and testing it later. As it is a continuous process, the make and test and learn approach does better. Also taking manageable steps helps in diagnosing the problem or releasing the features in the product than creating a mammoth.

- The MVP that has gained traction with most customers should be proceeded with. Entrepreneurs launch many versions, but the one with the highest customers is the best. Most of the time the test and validation or some flaw in a business model also comes from the rivalry group which is also a good source to take on.

- Many founders are sceptical about idea theft while launching and testing an MVP. To be correct the value of testing the MVP outweigh the idea of theft. Some information could also be kept hidden while testing so that it does not have a reputation risk. Even if ideas are nothing until they are executed, entrepreneurs should work and focus more on execution and scaling up the venture rather than worrying about idea theft.

- Creating a constrained product will lead to users using only a subset of features. An entrepreneur should focus on the 'need to have features' at the initial stage rather than the 'nice to have features'. Fewer features will reduce complexity for an early adopter or basic user; features for the masses can be added once the MVP is solidified. Features are luxuries with costs involved. Similarly, a constrained operation is necessary to develop a solid base further. Iteration is a long step. Burdening any product with too many features without getting feedback has often led to mess and failure.

- During the initial phases, the founding team have limited details and data about the customer segment and other metrics. It is not clear which segment will prefer which features and what the product's future would be, so it's better to have a constraint. However, the early adopters who may be attracted to the product may need a unique selling position, without which the product does not meet the specification of unmet need.

- The constraints can also be put in the same way on the operational front when running a campaign across all social media. The entrepreneur should be selective and figure out where the customers are, which could be a better alternative than spilling all over. It also helps in getting feedback and spotting failure and channelizing success across the other platforms.

- A letter of intent is used which is signed for purchase by the customer for products that are not fully developed and operational. If a subsequent number of customers showed on the landing pages, then the hypothesis or MVP can be validated, and the entrepreneur can move forward. However, if the customer did not show up, then there is a need to look after the services that the entrepreneur is offering and do a proper diagnosis. This methodology not only validates the hypothesis but also gives reliable data and metrics like purchase commitment and generating funds.

## 8.2 Scaling the venture

Acquiring a large number of customers without validating the business model can be daunting hence constraining the customer initially is often a good way to fix the holes in the model. The usability test of around five customers is enough to gauge the business model up to 90%. Once solidified, the venture proposition and getting the green signal that the venture is a good product market fit, the venture is ready to scale. Verification means that customers liked the product, the product is well versed with the need, the market size is increasing, employees are willing to work and the venture has raised money which is the final indicator that the venture is ready to scale.

However, before concluding the business model should be stress tested for higher volumes and resources must be evaluated to gauge the real potential. Scaling is a double edge sword where too much load can lead to a crash while too much preparation and no response from the market can exhaust the resources. Premature scaling often hampers the organization and can be the last nail in the coffin. It is strongly advised that entrepreneurs should scale when the product market fit is analysed. Reiterating and changing the product proposition after you have millions of customers waiting for the product, could surely kill the Startup. Also, the gestation period for the Startup would be well thought out as too early can lead to immature abortion. Cash needed, cash flow and burn rate and resources, employees, infrastructure, research and development are much needed before scaling.

Google, is continuously evolving and adding new features and developing new products because they have the resources, team, budget and experts that can deal with them. On the other hand, an entrepreneur starts solo, without a team, and limited money makes the task cumbersome. What differentiates the two is the potential of the idea; given the same idea, google can do better but is so streamlined that thinking out of the box becomes difficult. Many businesses often have a network effect, which multiplies with the users on Facebook Twitter and Instagram. The process of iteration and development is continuous and hence, to gain traction and market share it is often suggested to take a big leap forward and scale. The validation of process and hypothesis testing is often a continuous process which is even executed by a large organization. However, Startups in many ways are new and noble which leaves a gap for improvement and risk of failure.

# 9. The blood of the business

## *9.1 Financing*

*VCs are your new bosses, how to tackle them and maintain control of the firm!*

A Startup when launched had to deal with many tasks. The preliminary task in new businesses is product creation, gaining customers, and assembling teams. Financing for a Startup is one of the crucial events for business success. Whether it is gathering seed capital from government sources or attracting VCs, entrepreneurial finance is the core part of the venture. Raising funds helps businesses streamline activities and provide much-needed resources to the business.

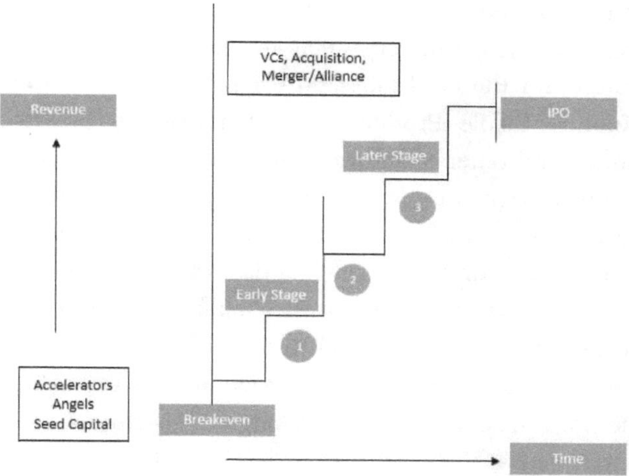


The industry an entrepreneur is operating could be decisive in funding. For example, the chances of getting funds are higher if a Startup is operating in software and biotechnology. Investors look for big market sizes with lucrative exits within five to seven years. Angel investors fund more than Venture Capitalists. Angel investors are more likely to fund at the seed stage than VCs. The stage of a Startup and the industry it is operating in also matter.

## 9.2 Advice on Money making and survival

1. You need a lot of money to start

It's a common misconception that entrepreneurs need tonnes of money to start. The advice would be to start small and invest incrementally in the business rather than waiting for the ideal time and big savings. The concept of Minimal Viable Product has often made it possible to launch and reiterate the value proposition of a business in a small segment. Stress testing before expanding the business to a small subset of the population is often wiser and needs much fewer funds. No business grows overnight, whether you invest a million dollars or a few bucks! The gestation period of the Startup will remain the same but you may need seed capital in both cases. Getting the proof of concept and checking the potential of an idea often needs low cash. If you have the proof, move forward, if you don't, reiterate it. The amount of money earned and tractions from customers show the potential of the business.

When you start big, with tonnes of cash and invest heavily in the project, it's difficult to roll back. With limited cash invested you have full control. If entrepreneurs have persistence and courage, then the business will grow but it will take time. Don't invest overnight! The gestation period may vary depending upon the business you choose.

1.   *All I need is VC money to get ahead*

VC see the Startups with a different lens, it's a money game. They have the skin in the game. Venture Capital financing has a vicious and virtual cycle. It's better to bootstrap than take outside money. External funding is related to ownership, raising a tonne of cash means diluting shares of the company. Subsequently, it also dilutes the culture of the company. The investor may focus on hiring and building a great culture for hyper-growth. The chain reaction occurs and the people you are hiring will be hiring and building teams, who do not actually understand the culture of the company. VCs bring professional management which leads to answering to someone else. For most, it defeats the purpose of starting the company.

Experts in the field argue about the rich vs king dilemma. Research says that the value of the companies that go to the rich approach is approximately three times higher than those that choose the king's way. Rich means accepting outside funds which come with VC; and the king is all about the control of the company which limits the outside investment hence, the stake of the Startup remains within the control of the founder. But entrepreneurs should ask the basic question, 'why did I start a company?' Is it with the thought of gaining a lot of money, or is it because of the  self-satisfaction of running a company? I am a firm believer that many start businesses because they want to control, they want to be their own boss.

Also, if you need a lot of money, you will be constantly focused on fundraising instead of focusing on the business. Founders may think they started the business because of love of the product and the company but that is going to be spent on finance instead. When you are taking money at an early stage the pre-money evaluation is going to destroy the Startup from a financial perspective. The second factor to consider is dividends. Once you have series B on top of series A, and series C on top of series B, you have a compounding effect of all and the dividends eat your equity. It will take cash and we all know the power of compounding.

The positive is that VCs are under-compensated for the risk that they are taking. The strongest position that founders can take in any negotiation is the position of indifference. When you are in cash flow breakeven you are indifferent, whether you take money or not, it is not going to impact the business, as the business is cash flow positive. So, the final say is bootstrapping over VC funding. In certain industries, you need so much money to begin, that you need VCs like drug development or chip manufacturing. So, the founders can run the company where it is profitable enough so that they could get a private equity firm to come in and buy a piece of the company. This is called dividend recap which is selling some of the company to firms.

How the hell our mean weight just became the thrice of my weight?

### 9.3 Deciding the Capital need

The answer to the question 'how much cash is needed?' depends upon various factors like the stage in which the business is operating, which could be ideation, pilot testing, customer acquisition, or stress testing to name a few. The second factor to consider is the industry in which the business is operating. For example, the need for funds in a service sector may differ from that of manufacturing. Manufacturing based businesses require heavy machinery, inventory, land and assets which are more capital intensive than SaaS based product businesses.

The pace of growth is another factor. Higher the pace of the growth the more cash intensive the business will be. To sum it up, of the above factors, the stage of the Startup, industry of operation, and pace of growth are vital when deciding the need for capital. The point to note is initial financing is too costly for entrepreneurs in the form of losing a lot of equity. However, as the business becomes proven, it has better bargaining power. To gain the edge over the investor when raising capital, make sure you have enough cash, so that founders are indifferent to the end result. A desperate need for cash may end up giving too much equity and a low valuation of the company. Also, talking with multiple investors at the same time keeps the funding perspective in the favour of the entrepreneur.

Asset intensity is important to consider when deciding the amount of funding. The capital requirement is dependent upon technology, machinery, employees and marketing expenses. The financial tool for an entrepreneur to gauge the amount of funding is cumulated cash flow analysis. The expected working capital and monthly fixed cost are two factors to consider as they can erode and heighten the capital requirement.

As explained above the assent intensity, profitability and rate of growth are a few more important factors to gauge the potential business finance need. When businesses start there is hardly any profit so it could be considered zero, secondly the rate of growth could be kept at 30%.

Free cash flow = assumed profit − asset intensity ratio. Growth rate

1+ growth rate

The high-intensity ratio businesses have negative cash flow as opposed to the SaaS based business models that have positive cash flow due to low asset intensity. The rate of growth equally affects the cash flow; the higher growth rate can turn the business's cash flow positive while the low growth can make a negative cash flow.

### 9.4 How to decide which funding is suitable?
*A trade-off between the funding options*

The debt investor is risk averse but the equity investor looks for a money multiplier effect and is ready to take a substantial amount of risk. Both types of investors pitch their interest, debt investors will pitch for stable return, while equity will encourage risky but maximum return. An investor can have a profound impact on the growth trajectory of the Startup.

*Debt*

Debt investment is raised through traditional channels like banks which lend money at a fixed term interest rate. The major benefit of debt investment is founders only pay interest and the principal loan amount, in a fixed time. Even if the business is extremely successful, banks do not get the share. Debt investors take collateral security (which works when the loan amount gets defaulted) and take a calculated or proven risk for businesses which sometimes makes the businesses inclined toward the established businesses rather than new ideas. In addition, banks also seek businesses that are cash flow positive, can cover the business interest, and are less risky.

*Equity*

Entrepreneurs give up a major chunk of equity raising through this method. When Startups become successful, the equity given can cost multiple times. Equity capital is expensive. Every time an entrepreneur raises it, they dilute the shares of the company. Equity investors such as VCs and angels receive a long-term ownership stake in the business venture in lieu of money invested. The risk of the equity investor is substantial in comparison to the debt investor. In case of failure, the equity investor will lose everything at the same time they also enjoy tremendous upside potential.

Innovative companies often rely on equity rather than debt. Equity investors not only bear risk but also provide good mentorship and advisee support to the Startups. Equity investors diversify the risk by diversifying their portfolio of companies.

*Cash Flow Financing*

Some lenders allow businesses to lend debt against their capability to generate cash. It is mostly available by commercial banks however; finance companies and loan institutions can also use this method to finance the business. Account receivable from the creditworthy customer can be used to finance the venture which is usually less than 90%. A detailed analysis is also needed before funding but it lives a gap of manipulation. Similarly, inventory, equipment and real estate which is usually fifty to 80% can also be financed. A letter of credit is given which is like a bank guarantee that the company can use to purchase goods. It is more like a credit card which allows purchasing goods in form of commitment. Asset-based financing is used by banks and when one defaults, these assets can be seized. Also, a patent is generally tied to the success or failure of a business. So, patents fail to convince the lender and are generally not considered for financing.

# *Type of Business and Financing: Finance Framework*

| Capital Requirement | High | Proven Technologies (Capital Intensive) | New Technology (Capital Intensive) |
|---|---|---|---|
| | Low | *Small Business* | *New Technology* |
| | | *Low* | **High** |
| | | *Newness/Innovation* | |

- Small business-like restaurants and auto parts manufacturers require low capital with limited innovation and are dependent on personal credit and bank loans for funds. Debt funding is the traditional way which is often better to go with limited interest.

- Capital intensive and proven technology-based businesses like powerplants, infrastructure development projects, and well-developed technologies look for commercial banks and strategic investors. While high capital-intensive companies which have innovative offerings are hard to fund and often seek government support.

- The new technologies look for angels and VCs to meet the need. There is a high level of uncertainty which will not be bought by the traditional debt investors. Often the technologies or innovation is unverifiable and has uncertainty that defers the debt investor from funding. Many entrepreneurs don't have the collateral to get a loan from banks. Also, they look for aggressive growth which is more suited for angels and VCs. The above figure provides the financial framework for the capital requirement.

### 9.5 Types of equity investors: Venture Capitalist
### Venture Capitalist

Entrepreneurs meet the financing need from family, bootstrapping, bank loans, or angels and Venture Capitalists (VC). It is important to consider the structure of the VCs and angels in funding Startups. The organizational structure of VC investors is limited to partners, and they put cash into the VC fund. VC funds invest in entrepreneurs in lieu of equity which gives returns to investors over a period. VCs are partnerships and they raise their own funds. They also manage monetary inflow from limited partners (institutional investors, pension funds, and limited universities). VCs invest in a startup hoping for a large return which can be converted into cash, by selling the equity of the company. VCs make money in two ways first is management fees which are fixed at one to 3% per year (90% of VC firms charge 2% a year). And the second way to earn is profit share which is about 20% of fund performance.

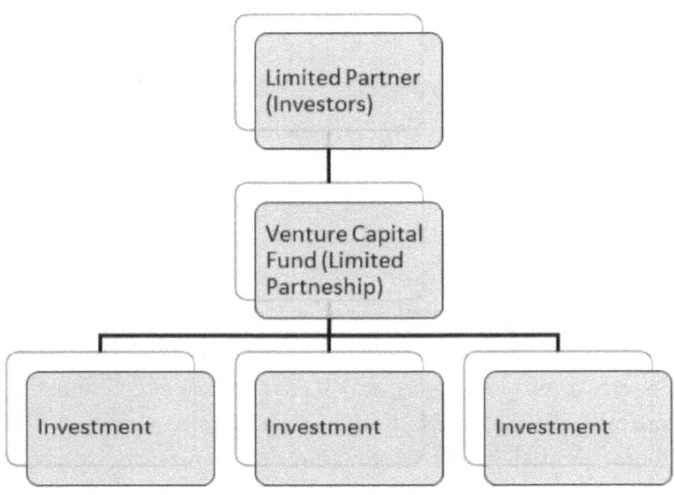


The VCs are professionally managed and do due diligence before investing. It is often wise to consider the VC portfolio before seeking funds. Some venture capitalists are more inclined toward the Startups of certain industries. The normal fund size for VCs is +2 million. Once VCs agree to fund a Startup, they add value through network, governance and guidance. Their fund size is +100 million. The funding businesses are based on the portfolio of companies rather than relying on one business. Not all the businesses they invest in will fail or succeed. Some make a good profit while some fail. An important strategy of VC funding is to bet on the right venture and make enough investments that can be cashed as a successful exit. The irony is that more than 50% of businesses' VCs fund fail. Hence, all the bet is on the few ventures and the valuation of the business during the exit. The success of VCs is heavily dependent upon their success to cover the losses.

VCs also balance the act of funding by not giving too much weightage to a single venture at the same time by funding adequately. Adequate funds are the butter in case of the successful exit of the business. To counter the steep failure, venture businesses often raise several rounds of funding which is beneficial for both the entrepreneurs and capitalists. The key task VCs are good at performing, is identifying the ventures that will fail and shifting the resources to other potential business ideas. Most failures and successes are indeed in the portfolio of the VCs.

Venture capitalists are often looking for $50 million to $100 million in five to seven years. Entrepreneurs who are king often look for an alternative to VCs, as VCs comes with the control right, including the board of director, they do have the power to merge, sell assets and even replace the CEO through voting rights. If the VCs feel that the founder does not have the capability to meet the existing demand, they can replace him or her. The VC's judgement to fund a Startup is not based on data. Unfortunately, when dealing with individuals we also have to face the hard truth of biasedness in ethnicity, gender and age. According to statistics, women are less likely to receive funding from all sources and only 3.5% of VC backed firms have identifiable female founders.

# VC Vs Angels Vs Super Angels Vs Seed Incubators

|  | Venture Capitalist | Angel | Super Angel | Seed Incubator | Crowdfunding |
|---|---|---|---|---|---|
| Funding | Limited Partners | Self | Depends | Depends | Many 6yh |
| Stage of Interest | Round A | Seed | Seed | Pre-Seed | Pre-Seed |
| Amount of Investment | $2M+ | $ 25,000-$ 500,000+ | Depends | $20,000-$100,000 | $100-$1M |
| Value Addition | Networks, Governance, Guidance | Sometimes | Networks, Governance, Guidance | Initial mentoring, Networks | Indirect |
| Fund Size | $100M+ | NA | $10M-$70M | $10M-$30M | NA |
| How they make money | Fees and carry leading to large exits | Equity leading to any exit | Equity leading to any exit, fees | 5% -10% equity | They don't / They will |

## 9.6 Equity investor: Angels
*Angels of dreams!*

Angels are individuals or groups of individuals who invest earned or saved money in a start-up. The individuality in nature of angels brings tremendous heterogeneity and they are managed personally rather than professionally. Angel investors fund the startups through their own hard earned cash. They provide seed capital and the average amount of investment is between $25,000 - $500,000. Angel investors add value through guidance and get revenue through exits.

If the money required is less than one million, then it is better to look for angels than VCs. While VCs on the other hand meet the heavy funding need. Many entrepreneurs may have an existing relationship with the angel which reduces the due diligence. Angels provide less structure to the existing businesses. However, they do provide enough thrust to convert the raw idea to gain momentum and attract VC investment. Angles also invest without the tight control of the company, due diligence, and time limit of exit.

Angels are heterogeneous and come in different shapes and sizes. One may have deep domain expertise while the other may have network connections, hiring capabilities and business acumen. Angels are generally former entrepreneurs with successful exits or raised IPO which support the spirit of the entrepreneur and look for thrill and excitement. They also act as a helping hand to fellow animals and see funding as a philanthropic act at the same time having an economic expectation. Many entrepreneurs avoid VCs and like to prefer freedom rather than due diligence. Angels are difficult to find, websites like Angellist had made it easy for entrepreneurs to connect, meet and raise funds. There had been a surge in angel investment.

*Other Investors*

Private companies and corporations also invest in Startups. The structure of the investing resembles that with the VCs. They have operational managers who work and build a portfolio for corporations. They invest in startups with dual motives, one with the intent to acquire new technology, idea, or team or gain competitive insight, and secondly, for handsome exits post evaluation. This type of strategic investor differs in the size of the investment. They have a deep pocket, infrastructure and core advantage which makes them different from the VC's investment.

Startups often have to find the sweet spot in the organization where they can contribute and add value to the existing firm and manage harmony between the Startup and its partner organizations. It also opens the door to buy-out clauses but with limitations like the limit/cap on the return of the entrepreneur employees which cannot exceed the payment received by the CEO of the partner organizations.

### *9.7 How to reach the VCs?*

The first step to getting the right person who can fund your venture is casual dating. Try to meet as many VCs as possible through your network and hang out in social gatherings. Nowadays it is very easy to get connected to potential funders through social media platforms like LinkedIn. The second step is proof point timing and keeps spreading the good news about what your company does and where about. In the next step, entrepreneurs can scrutinize interest, and check if they have an interest in your company. Many of them may not have an interest and hence, checking the interest of people, helps. Also, VCs and angels may have their portfolios tilted toward one or another. Entrepreneurs may have to sit down and look at potential funders and figure out who might be most interested. Finally, craft an alternative, by starting to cut less desirable partners, who are least likely to fund.

Entrepreneurs need a tool kit for pitching. The first of these tools is the elevator pitch. Before the pitch send an email with a ten to twelve-slide presentation and an executive summary of your business plan to your potential investor. You never send a complete business plan. The content of the presentation is the first thing that gives an overview and hooks the audience.

During face-to-face combat with VCs, an entrepreneur should have the ten to twelve slides ready and give a demo of what you have to offer. Entrepreneurs who get funded are good storytellers; indicating things that you have a personal connection with, such as not drawing a large salary, mentioning MBA, and mentioning a previous employer attract the audience and investor. Having a clear process is another factor for better pitches. For example, show awards and prototypes or prestigious ties that get personal attention. A talented team and strong ties from the industry and corporations help gain credibility.

## 9.8 Term sheet and Financing Structure

*Let's get the legal pros and cons!*

Many of the provision of the term sheet enables the investors and entrepreneur to classify risk and reward. The three noticeable features of a term sheet are valuation, control and risk. Valuation is a negotiated outcome when the deal is made between the financer and the entrepreneur. It also involves the bargaining power of the parties involved. Hence, valuation is very subjective in nature. If done appropriately, it can stimulate a million dollars, if it doesn't, it is just vague. An entrepreneur should focus equally on both the deal terms and the valuation. The funding is not the end result of any Startup, it's just a mechanism to move the Startup from phase A to B. Equally important are the deal terms. If not negotiated properly, they can have a devastating end result, even the firing of the founder.

Specialised experts in VC funding are needed. It is often suggested to talk to lawyers before entering into any formal agreement. A more in-depth review of the term sheet is often needed before signing it. The major theme that should be looked at before entering into an agreement is valuation, control and legal bounding. *National Venture Capital Association* and *European Venture Capital Association* often provide good definitions and sample term sheets for reference.

### 9.9 Convertible financing structure

Convertible preferred stock is the most common financing instrument that a VC generally considers as a common class of equity. Financing instruments have equity debt conversion features. Upon reaching the liquidity event like IPO, acquisition or bankruptcy, holders of convertible preferred stock can redeem them at the face value or convert their stock as common stock to get a share of the company. The flexibility of converting equity to debt is a win-win situation for the investor. In the case of low valuation, the shareholder redeems the debt investment and in the case of higher valuation, the shareholder converts to equity and gets a share in the company which will be greater than the face value of the investment.

The investor can have the share in three major forms – pure equity, convertible -non-participating preferred stock, and convertible preferred stock. The other form of financial instrument is the convertible note also known as convertible debt. These instruments are used in seed rounds or early stages of the Startup and are commonly preferred by the angels. They are a non-priced round of financing which means that there is no valuation assigned to the company.

### 9.10 Derisk the deal and increase the valuation

Entrepreneurs should raise money in stages, which means there had to be a gap in raising funds. The time in between stages is a better way to fix the holes in the businesses and run experiments. Enough money should also be raised to reach the next milestone. The valuation of the Startup should go up in between the buffer zone of raising funds but it can also go down dramatically. Entrepreneurs should make sure that they do the homework to fix the company perspective and get customers which will move the business forward. When raising the funds, the startup should always focus on de-risking the deal, which will eventually increase the valuation of the startup. A significant gap between the times of raising the funding is useful. The equation is simple, de-risk the deal and increases the valuation.

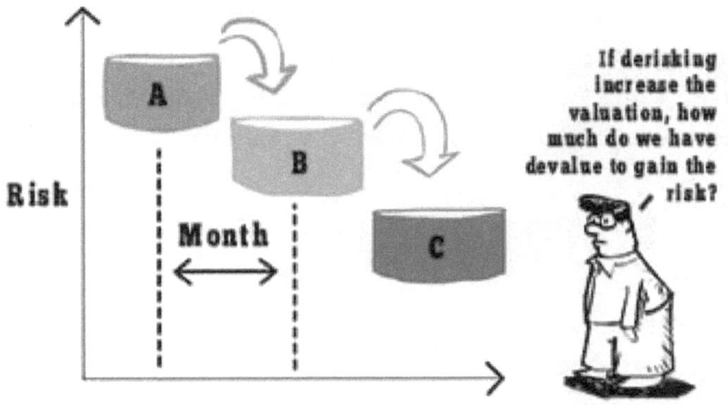

When using staging as a process, consider a small amount of investment early, foolproofing the business increases the valuation and raises the next round of funding. This process is used both by VCs and entrepreneurs as the chances of failing can make them take a separate path. While getting the initial traction VCs pay more amount of funds and at the same time entrepreneurs also save millions of dollars. The key to note is VCs rarely fund the business in one go. They just give entrepreneurs enough money to sustain and concretise the business. Many entrepreneurs are also sceptical about raising equity funding until they have a proven market and product that meet the demand of a target segment.

The above figure shows the strategies in different Startup phases. Initially, during the first six-month, friends and family help to start the project. The entrepreneurs should focus next on the prototyping of the model. They can also bootstrap and look for angel funding in the meantime. The next stages would be product development, deployment and proliferation of the business when the founder could raise series A, B and C rounds of funding between fifteen to twenty-four months of startup initiation.

*Stage and need for funding*

| *Homework* | *Prototype* | *Product Development* | *Deployment* | proliferation |
| --- | --- | --- | --- | --- |
| *F&F* | *Bootstrap Or Angel* | *Series A* | *Series B* | Series C |
| *6 months* | *6-12 months* | *15-24 months* | *18-24 months* | |

### 9.11 Accelerators

Accelerators have become an important part of the Startup ecosystem which fund, guide, provide logistical support and equip the founders with access to investors. These are for-profit enterprises. The entrepreneur applies and pitches their venture through a formal application process among thousands of applications. In lieu of the support, accelerators take equity of around 6 to 10% in the venture. There are limited numbers of spots in the accelerators. The accelerators have an extensive network in form of yearly cohorts. Even alumni, advisors, and board members associated with accelerators often make the lonely journey encouraging. Upon selection, entrepreneurs carry a brand which adds value to the Startup. Not all accelerators carry the same brand name and add value, entrepreneurs are advised to be selective when applying for an accelerator.

Many accelerators work in a niche area. Accelerators help in developing a prototype and come into play before the pre-seed stage of the Startup. The two models for accelerators that had been successful are Techstar and Y-combinator. Y-combinator is an intense, everything at one place programme. Getting selected into incubators will get the money and the chances increases, to succeed or fail quickly. Startups through accelerators also get funds faster and a majority are likely to fail. If you can make it to the top tier of accelerators it is helpful, which gives the much needed help at that stage.

*2019's Most Active Angel & Seed-Stage Investors, Globally*

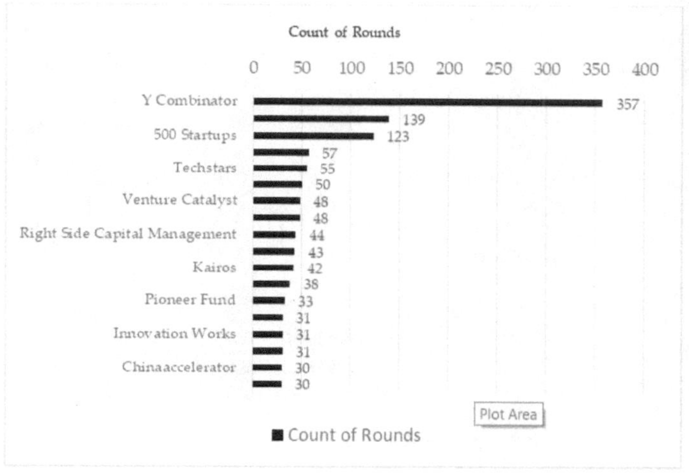


*Source: https://news.crunchbase.com/news/the-q4-eoy-2019-global-vc-report-a-strong-end-to-a-good-but-not-fantastic-year/*

## 9.12 Crowdfunding

*Its short IPO is a good way to gather a few bucks for Startups.*

Crowdfunding platforms help entrepreneurs raise the funds through crowd platforms by offering their products. Kickstarter and Indiegogo are the two most common sources of the platform that are used widely. The model allows a large number of people to invest a small amount by purchasing the product that helps to get the initial cash for Startups. Crowdfunding fills the gap in the financing ecosystem. At the same time, it also builds a customer base which many entrepreneurs need when starting up.

Crowdfunding distributes the risk from a few handfuls of people to the masses. Crowdfunding is regulated in various countries however it is still unregulated in many others which may impose challenges in raising funds. Also, the community for it is well spread among various countries.

Delay in shipment or product manufacturing is most common, which hampers the credibility of the Startup. A well-planned launch is good for both Startups and customers.

Since the business had to be funded by not one but many individuals the chances of mass judgement in deciding the success are crucial. The higher support from the crowdfunding signals success at least in the initial stage. This helps in getting the much-needed support, design and feedback in product development. It also builds the sales funnels, and initial customer bases and develop a feedback mechanism to fix any error in product development. Crowdfunding has an emotional appeal which attracts people to contribute to the cause.

In some industries specifically art, community-based businesses receive support from fellow participants and members that help bring a great product. Many businesses did not get any support from crowdfunding at all. The social network of the inventor for the crowdfunding matters and it is more than just cash. Crowdfunded projects signal the quality of endorsement, team with experience, prototype, and detailed planned blueprint. Above all, when seeking funding support, minute details like spelling errors and frequency of updates about the concept development matter. It helps connect the founder through videos, pictures, and how they get started to the globe.

Women are doing far better than men in crowdfunding technological ventures. They outperform men by 13%, mostly driven by tech projects. Women have a strong network and moral support system from fellow members who help in gaining initial traction.. Most women are supported by other fellow women. The activist women as common friends to women entrepreneurs, work as a catalyst and are more likely to say good things about the projects than their male counterparts, as well as, spread goodwill.

Women specifically are skewed towards other women, so they help other women out. It turns out that it is not the case with men. Crowdfunding works well if the entrepreneur is already part of a greater community. If you are part of a network that cares a lot about you and your innovation the chances are higher that you will be backed up. When you are already part of the network and you know what the need of the market is, you are in a really good position to do the project. The crowdfunded project that raised the highest money is films about drones.

## 9.13 How to launch a crowdfunding campaign

- Write your pitch and practise it before making the pitch. In the case of video pitches, preparing a written script before recording a video helps in minimizing mistakes and boosts confidence. Hire a professional who can make a professional video, it will pay back.

- Provide supportive credentials like educational qualification, MNC Company you had worked with or any other association that gives recognition!

- Showcase of prototype/product in written documents, websites, images or videos rather than just pitching empty-handed; it helps increase the credibility and show the preparedness of the entrepreneur.

- Make sure to come to point of sale with an offering, not more than two minutes after you start the video.

- Don't forget to connect with the masses by sharing your personal details, and what they might have in common with you like community, geography, or pain points.

- Promote fundraising campaigns across social media. Paid advertising can be a way to get initial traction.

- Began your pitch with a story, for example, I had X problem and I was so stressed! It catches the attention of listeners and also tells why this problem matters and how you are putting effort to solve it.

- Know your target segment, and design your pitch specifically keeping the segment in mind. You can consider demography, social status, education level, income and geography to custom tune the message!

- Friends, family and fools are the early customers, tap them well; reach them asking to support your initiative!

- Getting the initial support/funders will require the most effort. If the project isn't able to create a buzz, it is likely to fail.

- Plan carefully the attribute of products, shipping cost of products, mechanism to ship overseas and accessories with the product.

- Properly gauge the capacity to produce the product/offer within a time frame; a delay in shipping can get bad reviews that can hurt the campaign.

# About Author

Subhash Kumar is an alumnus of XLRI Jamshedpur. He had completed PGP in entrepreneurship from XLRI Jamshedpur, after pursuing graduation and post-graduation from Banaras Hindu University (BHU). He belongs to Bokaro Steel City in Jharkhand. He has been an entrepreneur and the art of creation fascinates him. He has a decade experience in professional and entrepreneurial field. He had worked with companies like Planning Commission, E&Y, CM Office and IIM Ahmedabad. Presently, He is working working NBFC based out of Jaipur, Rajasthan.